What Girls Need to Know about Guys

Other products by
JOHN HILTON III

Books

Why? Powerful Answers and Practical Reasons for Living LDS Standards
(coauthored with Anthony Sweat)

How? Essential Skills for Living the Gospel
(coauthored with Anthony Sweat)

I Lost My Phone Number, Can I Have Yours?

Please Pass the Scriptures

The Little Book of Book of Mormon Evidences

CDs

Dating and the Plan of Happiness

The Dog Ate My Scriptures

I Can Do Hard Things

DVDs

Isn't Being Good Good Enough?

Why? Powerful Answers and Practical Reasons for Living LDS Standards
(with Anthony Sweat)

What Girls Need to Know about Guys

John Hilton III
Lani O. Hilton

Salt Lake City, Utah

To our children, with love

Illustrations by Bryan Beach; © 2011 Deseret Book
Photos on page 3 by Lani Hilton

© 2011 John Hilton III and Lani Hilton

All rights reserved. No part of this book may be reproduced in any form or by any means without permission in writing from the publisher, Deseret Book Company, P. O. Box 30178, Salt Lake City, Utah 84130. This work is not an official publication of The Church of Jesus Christ of Latter-day Saints. The views expressed herein are the responsibility of the authors and do not necessarily represent the position of the Church or of Deseret Book Company.

DESERET BOOK is a registered trademark of Deseret Book Company.

Visit us at DeseretBook.com

Library of Congress Cataloging-in-Publication Data
Hilton, John, III, author.
  What guys need to know about girls; what girls need to know about guys / John Hilton III, Lani O. Hilton.
    p. cm.
  Includes bibliographical references.
  ISBN 978-1-60908-054-9 (paperbound)
  1. Man-woman relationships—Religious aspects—The Church of Jesus Christ of Latter-day Saints.
  2. Dating (Social customs)—Religious aspects—The Church of Jesus Christ of Latter-day Saints.
  I. Hilton, Lani, author. II. Title.
  BX8643.Y6H5457 2011
  241'.6765088289332—dc22   2011001900

Printed in the United States of America
Malloy Lithographing Inc., Ann Arbor, Michigan
10   9   8   7   6   5   4   3   2   1

Contents

Acknowledgments vii

Introduction 1

1. What Girls Need to Know about Girls 5

2. Discover Who You Really Are 12

3. Four Things You Should Know about Boys 19

4. A Topic You Might Not Want to Hear About 26

5. Expect (and Accept) the Respect 34

6. What about Kissing? 44

7. What Guys Wish Girls Knew 50

8. Potential Pitfalls 55

9. What Should She Do? 61

Conclusion 66

Date Night 69

Steps and Slides 70

Lani Olsen Hilton is the fifth of twelve children. She was born in Hawaii and grew up in San Diego, California. She graduated from Brigham Young University with a degree in family life education and a minor in music. She loves being married, raising her children, and teaching gospel truths to youth, adults, and children. Some of her favorite high school memories are running cross country, taking a dance class with her mom, hiking Mt. Whitney with her siblings, and leading service clubs.

John Hilton III was born in San Francisco and grew up in Seattle. In high school, he played tennis, snowboarded, worked as a lifeguard, and participated in drama productions. He served an LDS mission in Denver, and got a bachelor's degree from Brigham Young University. He earned a master's degree from Harvard and a PhD from BYU, both in education. He has taught seminary and institute and spoken at BYU Education Week and EFY. One lesser-known fact about John is that in high school he won a pizza-eating contest, eating twenty-two pieces of pizza (they were small pieces ☺).

John and Lani have lived in Boise, Boston, Mexico, Miami, and, currently, Utah. They are the parents of five children.

Acknowledgments

First, we want to acknowledge the many people at Deseret Book whose help we are very grateful for: Chris Schoebinger, who had the original concept for this book; Leslie Stitt, who has blessed this project as editor; Heidi Taylor, for her creative contributions; Tonya Facemyer, for supervising the typesetting; and Heather Ward, who was invaluable with the design and layout. Thanks also to Bryan Beach for the awesome illustrations.

We also thank the hundreds of youth who have helped us refine the ideas in this book. Whether it was honestly sharing with us your point of view, telling us experiences you've had, or simply talking together about these issues, your thoughts have helped shape this book.

Special gratitude is due to the youth who reviewed drafts of this book, including Alex, Ashleigh, Eleni, Erika, Jacob, Jordan, Josh, Karen, Kelsey, Kierstyn, Loyda, Mina, Nicki, Rachel, Spencer, and Taylor.

Finally, special thanks to the literally thousands of young women and young men for the great examples you set in living the principles of the gospel as you interact with one another. Your kind actions will have a profound influence for years to come in the lives of your friends, the people you date, and those who quietly observe you.

Introduction

Lani — Hi, girls! It's me, Lani (rhymes with Bonnie) Hilton.

John — And I'm John Hilton III. The young women of the Church are so amazing! A few months after my wife, Lani, and I were married, a member of the bishopric asked to visit us in our home. I was excited, because I assumed he was going to give us a calling.

When he came over, we talked for a few minutes, and then he said, "We have a calling for you. We'd like you to serve as the Mia Maid adviser."

I said, "I accept."

"Actually," he said, "I was talking to your wife." :)

"Oh."

That was as close as I've ever gotten to serving in the Young Women organization—but I still have had many opportunities to be around the amazing young women of the Church.

To start out, I have two sisters and ten sisters-in-law! Lani's mom always says that there are no "in-laws" or "out-laws" in our family, so I always refer to each of these twelve women as my "sisters." Young women are important to me!

In addition, I have had many wonderful opportunities to speak directly to groups of young women. During the week at Especially for Youth, there is a time when the young men and young women separate.

Speaking with the young women is my favorite part of the week. You carry a marvelous spirit with you!

Of course, no matter how much I appreciate young women, I never have been and never will be one of them. So I knew from the beginning that I would need Lani's help in writing this book.

Lani—Back to me, Lani. I'm glad you're reading this book! I love young women! God has endowed women with especially wonderful qualities. I am so grateful for women, and I'm so glad I am a woman! Why are women wonderful? I remember friends complaining about the woes of childbirth years before they were even going to be mothers, or they complained about other physical things that accompany womanhood. Sometimes when you are going through a physical or emotional hardship, it is hard to see the glory in womanhood. But modern prophets want us to clearly understand the divine role of women. We hope as you read and reflect on the true principles in this book, the Spirit will testify to you of who you are. God lives. You are His daughter.

Proverbs 31 in the Old Testament talks about the value of women, particularly virtuous women. One thing it says is that the worth of a virtuous woman is far above rubies—or in other words, she is priceless. We hope that as you read this book and throughout your life, you will feel that you are priceless . . . because you are. God loves His daughters!

A Haircut

John—I usually cut my own hair, and then Lani finishes the back and sides. One afternoon I was getting ready to give myself a haircut when I was distracted by my children. After they quieted down, I began to give myself a haircut. It took only half a second for me to realize that something was wrong—I had forgotten to put on the attachment! I had created a bald spot on my head!

"Dad's in trouble!" my kids said, as they went to tell Mom.

When Lani came in, she was shocked. "You can't go out like that," she said. So she got a permanent marker and colored in the bald spot. But that just made it look like I had stitches.

Then she suggested taking some of the hair that we cut off and super gluing it to my head. It sounds crazy, I know, but it worked! I had a "hair patch."

My point in telling the haircutting story is that it illustrates that Lani is a true friend to me. She didn't want me to be embarrassed because of my haircut. Lani and I want to write to you as friends. We hope that this book will be a conversation just between us—as true friends.

James 1:22 says, "Be ye *doers* of the word, and not hearers only" (emphasis added). It's good for you to read this book, but it's even better to act on what you read. At the end of each chapter you will find a "James 1:22 Checklist" with some suggestions of things you could do to act on the principles we've discussed in that particular chapter.

Chapter 1

What Girls Need to Know about Girls

Lani — We're excited to talk to you about boys. But before you can really understand the opposite gender, you should first understand who you really are. The more confident you are with yourself, the more confident you will be interacting with guys. You are a daughter of your Heavenly Father, who loves you and wants you to be happy. Stop for a minute and let that sink in. Read the highlighted sentence <u>again</u> and let a smile come to your face. It is true. He wants you to live to your fullest potential and understand your divine nature as a daughter of God. When you really understand that principle, it will change how you relate to boys. It will change <u>everything</u> about your life. Maybe we can introduce this with a story.

JOHN — On my mission, my companion and I were tracting one evening when we came to a home with a fence around it. There was a sign on the fence that said, "Beware of Dog." We shook the gate to see if a dog would bark. Nothing happened. We rattled the gate even louder, but no dog came—so we opened the gate and walked into the yard.

The gate swung shut behind us as we walked toward the door. I was a couple of steps in front of my companion when we heard a loud barking noise. A giant dog came running around the side of the house.

My companion turned and ran for the fence. He began climbing it, and the dog was jumping up, trying to grab his feet. But my companion made it over the fence and was safe. I, on the other hand, was in trouble. The dog was between me and the fence. I could see no other escape, so I ran toward the front door and (without knocking) opened it.

"Help!" I yelled. "Help!"

A large man came running down the stairs, shouting at the dog.

When the dog calmed down, the man turned and bellowed at me, "What are you doing in my house?"

I didn't know what to say, so I just said, "Well, we were just trying to share a spiritual message . . ."

He cut me off. "I'm not interested!"

And that was fine with me because I was just happy to get out of there alive. Then the man said, "What's the matter with you? Can't you read?"

And he had a point. The sign, "Beware of Dog," was clear, but my companion and I chose to ignore it, thinking that we knew better.

We share this story with you because we feel that the subject of this chapter is like the sign, "Beware of Dog." Most of what we want to tell you about what girls need to know about girls is plain and obvious. But sometimes it seems so simple, it is overlooked.

Lani — But we cannot fail to overlook what it means for us to be women. The world would have you believe that you're "just a girl" or that women are second-class citizens in the world or in the Church. That is absolutely not true. One of the most important things young women need to understand is how valuable they really are. Consider these words from Elder Jeffrey R. Holland:

> I want you to be proud you are a woman. I want you to feel the reality of what that means, to know who you truly are. You are literally a spirit daughter of heavenly parents with a divine nature and an eternal destiny.

What Girls Need to Know about Guys

That surpassing truth should be fixed deep in your soul and be fundamental to every decision you make as you grow into mature womanhood.[1]

So, there are four calls to action from Elder Holland:
1. BE PROUD you are a woman.
2. FEEL what that means.
3. KNOW who you truly are.
4. MAKE SURE that truth is *fixed deep* in your soul and is *fundamental* to your every decision.

I can tell you that as I have done these four things, I have been blessed with happiness and confidence.

Another favorite quote of mine comes from President Gordon B. Hinckley:

Woman is God's **supreme** creation. Only after the earth had been formed, after the day had been separated from the night, after the waters had been divided from the land, after vegetation and animal life had been created, and after man had been placed on the earth, was woman created; and only then was the work pronounced complete and good.

Of all the creations of the Almighty, there is none more beautiful, none more inspiring than a lovely daughter of God who walks in virtue with an understanding of why she should do so, who honors and respects her body as a thing sacred and divine, who cultivates her mind and constantly enlarges the horizon of her understanding, who nurtures her spirit with everlasting truth.[2]

POWER QUOTE

Ladies, do we comprehend the value that our Heavenly Father places on our womanhood? We can change the world! Let me share a few stories about some of my favorite, but lesser-known women from the scriptures. Their names may sound funny, but they were women like you—and they changed the world.

Shiphrah and Puah were midwives who lived at the time that the Israelites were slaves to the Egyptians. The pharaoh was worried about the Israelites becoming too powerful, and so he told the midwives to kill all of the male babies they delivered. Can you imagine the pressure they were under? This wasn't peer pressure, this was pharaoh pressure!

But these women honored God more than the pharaoh and saved the male babies even though they knew the pharaoh would be angry with them.

Another woman named Jochebed lived during the same time period. She gave birth to a son and hid him from the Egyptian soldiers at great personal danger, since it was going against the pharaoh's wishes. As the boy grew older, she boldly conceived of a plan to save his life. Her daughter, Miriam, assisted in the plan and, consequently, Moses' life was saved. Think of it! The entire Old Testament was shaped because of the dedication of Shiphrah, Puah, Jochebed, and Miriam (see Exodus 1–2).

Some of my favorite women in the scriptures are ones who were anonymous. In Abraham 1:11 we read of three young women who "were offered up [to idols] because of their virtue; they would not bow down to worship gods of wood or of stone." These young women likely knew that life would not be easy for them if they chose to remain virtuous, but they did it anyway.

Women have a rich legacy in the scriptures. The first of Jesus' recorded miracles was performed for His own mother (John 2:1–11), and one of my favorite parts of the scriptural accounts of Christ's crucifixion and resurrection is that the first person to see the resurrected Savior was a woman (Mark 16:9). I hope that when you think of your womanhood, you feel good in your heart. I know God loves and honors women.

JOHN—When I think about the power a young woman has, I think of my great-great-great-grandmother Jane. She changed her life (and, consequently, mine) when she was just seventeen years old. Sometime during the 1840s, Jane Mathers and some of her family members were baptized in Michigan by LDS missionaries. Shortly after her family was baptized, Joseph Smith was martyred and Brigham Young became the leader of the Church, and he called for all the Saints to move to Nauvoo.

The Mathers family packed their wagon and prepared to travel to Nauvoo. The night before they were supposed to leave, a neighbor came and tried to persuade Jane's father that Mormonism was a wicked religion. The next morning, Jane's father announced,

My dear sisters, we believe in you. We believe in and are counting on your goodness and your strength, your propensity for virtue and valor, your kindness and courage, your strength and resilience.... We believe that God's plan is for you to become queens and to receive the highest blessings any woman can receive in time or eternity.... Never lose your precious identity by doing anything that would jeopardize the promised eternal future your Heavenly Father has provided for you.[3]

—Elder M. Russell Ballard

"The Mathers folk are not moving. We can live as good as we know how right here. We've got a good start here in Michigan."

Jane had a choice to make—should she stay with her family or follow the prophet? I wish I could have been there, watching her closely as she made up her mind. At last she decided. She packed a small bundle of personal things in a shawl. In my mind's eye I can see her hugging each family member, with tears in her eyes. With that, she set off for Nauvoo.

Jane never saw her family again. She went to Nauvoo and received her endowment in the Nauvoo Temple before traveling to Salt Lake City. She married and had just one child. But today her descendants are numbered in the hundreds. We are grateful that, as a young woman, she had the courage to follow the prophet.[4] You may not have to leave your family and walk across the plains, but you can bless generations to come as you walk away from the evils of the world.

You might be "only" a young woman—but be proud you are a woman. Jane Mathers, as a seventeen-year-old, made a choice that affected hundreds of people for eternity. You are making choices that affect many eternities—your own, and those of your friends and family.

I hope that you look at your womanhood as a treasured inheritance. Heavenly Father views you in a special way. Be proud that you are a woman. You are needed!

We love the movie *The Wizard of Oz*. And if you really think about it, there are some profound gospel insights in that movie. For example, consider the very last words spoken by the Wicked Witch of the West. After Dorothy throws water on her and she begins to melt, the witch says, "Who would have thought a good little girl like you could destroy my beautiful wickedness."[5] The truth is, righteous young women can destroy wickedness. As you use your influence for good, you will diminish the devil's power and strengthen those around you.

Elaine S. Dalton, as a counselor in the Young Women general presidency, once asked, "Can one righteous young woman change the world? The answer is a resounding 'yes!'"[6]

- Be proud you are a woman.
- You are God's supreme creation.
- What you do will affect tens of thousands, and even millions, in the generations to come.

Be Ye Doers of the Word

- Write in your journal about what it really means to you to be God's supreme creation.
- You've memorized the Young Women theme. Say it out loud to yourself. Use the first person ("I am a daughter..."). Really feel the meaning of the words.

THOUGHTS:
_____
_____
_____
_____
_____
_____
_____

Notes

1. Jeffrey R. Holland, "To Young Women," *Ensign*, November 2005, 28.
2. Gordon B. Hinckley, "Our Responsibility to Our Young Women," *Ensign*, September 1988, 11; emphasis added.
3. M. Russell Ballard, "Here Am I, Send Me," BYU devotional address, 13 March 2001; http://speeches.byu.edu/?act=viewitem&id=269; accessed 23 December 2010.
4. Ruth Naomi Savage Hilton, *My Grandmother Jane*, self-published. Copy in possession of authors.
5. "Melting the Wicked Witch," *The Wizard of Oz*, directed by King Vidor, et al. (Century City, CA: Metro-Goldwyn-Mayer [MGM], 1939), DVD.
6. Elaine S. Dalton, "It Shows in Your Face," *Ensign*, May 2006, 109.

Chapter 2

Discover Who You Really Are

Lani —I think I was really blessed as a young woman. I always felt confident in who I was as a daughter of God. But not everybody is so fortunate.

As a freshman in high school, Mollie felt like she had no friends at all. She had a hard time talking to other people, and her family had been having a lot of problems. She struggled with depression, and it seemed as though she couldn't do anything right. Even though other people told her she was beautiful, she felt ugly, both inside and out.

That began to change, though, when Mollie went to a youth conference. At this conference, she learned about who she was as a daughter of God. Even more important, she began to feel God's love for her. In this chapter, we want to share with you some of the things Mollie learned at that youth conference.

John— Elder Richard G. Scott said, "With all my capacity I encourage you to discover who you really are. I invite you to look beyond the daily routine of life. I urge you to discern through the Spirit your divinely given capacities. . . . Realize your full potential. Be the leader and example the Lord expects of you. . . . God loves you. I testify that as you seek His help, He will guide you to fulfill your worthy dreams."[1]

Think about that—have you discovered who you really are?

Sometimes it is easy to feel discouraged; maybe you have thought at

GREAT QUOTE

times that you are of little worth. If so, you're not alone. A lot of people, especially young women, it seems, go through times when they don't feel the divinity inside them. What makes this so tragic is that Satan wants us to feel this way. He doesn't want us to feel that we are children of God. Notice how the following scriptural exchange illustrates this principle.

In Moses 1, Moses had a marvelous vision in which he saw God. Our Father in Heaven said to Moses, "behold, thou art *my son*" (Moses 1:4; emphasis added). Later He said, "I have a work for thee, Moses, *my son*" (Moses 1:6; emphasis added). A third time He called Moses "my son" (Moses 1:7). Through this vision, Moses had a better understanding of his divine nature and relationship with God.

> My dear sisters, will you seek to remember with the help of the Holy Ghost who you are and who you have always been? Will you remember that you stood by our Savior without flinching? Remember that you were reserved for now because you would have the courage and determination to face the world at its worst and to help rear and lead a chosen generation. Remember the covenants you have made and the power they carry. Remember that you are noble and great and a potential heir of all our Father has. Remember that you are the daughter of a King.[2]
>
> —Sheri Dew

After this vision ended, Satan came, tempting Moses. In verse 12 he addressed Moses by calling him "*son of man*" (emphasis added). Isn't that interesting? God focused on the divinity in Moses ("my son"), but Satan tried to make Moses think only of his mortality.

Lani — Satan's tricks haven't changed today. He calls you "daughter of man," and tries to tempt you to focus on the things of the world. He wants you to believe that what you really are depends on your physical or worldly attributes. He whispers, "Unless you're beautiful (or lose

Be More Accepting of Yourself

"I plead with you young women to please be more accepting of yourselves, including your body shape and style, with a little less longing to look like someone else. We are all different. Some are tall, and some are short. Some are round, and some are thin. And almost everyone at some time or other wants to be something they are not . . . 'You can't live your life worrying that the world is staring at you. When you let people's opinions make you self-conscious you give away your power.'"[3]

—Elder Jeffrey R. Holland

"I am troubled by the practice of extreme makeovers. Happiness comes from accepting the bodies we have been given as divine gifts and enhancing our natural attributes, not from remaking our bodies after the image of the world. The Lord wants us to be made over—but in His image, not in the image of the world, by receiving His image in our countenances."[4]

—Susan W. Tanner

In one survey, 89 percent of boys said they were attracted to all types of girls, not just the "Sports Illustrated babe" types.[5] There is a whole lot more to you to like than just looks!

weight, or gain weight, or wear the right clothes, or are rich, etc.), you're worthless."

JOHN—Who you really are doesn't depend on how you look. Of course, it's important to be well-groomed, but what is really important is that you are the daughter of heavenly parents. They love you—and what else really matters? Remember that God called Moses "my son." He calls you "my daughter." He loves you. He knows your name. You are important to Him.

I think one of the greatest ways we can learn to understand who we really are is to worry less about ourselves and focus more on others. It sounds strange, but I've found that when I try to serve others and make them feel comfortable, I feel better about myself. On the contrary, when I think I need to focus more on myself, either on how I look or by bringing attention to myself, I don't feel as good about myself. LDS singer and presenter Hilary Weeks once said, "What matters isn't so much what I do to impress people, but how people feel when they are around me."[6] That's a powerful thought. As we reach out to help others we can better feel the truth about who we—and they—really are.

Susan W. Tanner, the former Young Women general president, taught something similar. She said:

> I remember well the insecurities I felt as a teenager with a bad case of acne. I tried to care for my skin properly. My parents helped me get medical attention. For years I even went without eating chocolate and all the greasy fast foods around which teens often socialize, but with no obvious healing consequences. It was difficult for me at that time to fully appreciate this body which was giving me so much grief. But my good mother taught me a higher law. Over and over she said to me, "You must do everything you can to make your appearance pleasing, but the minute you walk out the door,

Can you relate?

> **YOU CAN SOAR AS EAGLES!**
>
> You can soar as eagles and fly to heights not reached by your parents or grandparents. You can discover truths that will ignite your vision. You can challenge yourself to rise to greater levels of achievement. . . . How we love you. How we need you. You are the instruments the Lord has provided to work miracles that are urgently needed.[8]
> —Elder Richard G. Scott

forget yourself and start concentrating on others."[7]

Lani—I remember friends in high school who would head to the restroom after every class period to check their hair or reapply makeup. Or they would frequently pull out their little makeup mirrors during class. Remember Sister Tanner's mother's advice—"The minute you walk out the door, forget yourself and start concentrating on others." I was so happy during my high school years! In fact, some of my older brothers' friends nicknamed me "Smiley" for a while because they said they never saw me without a smile. I wore hand-me-down clothes, and I was not cool in many ways. But I attribute much of my happiness to the fact that I tried to focus on others. Every time since then when I have reached out to others, even at a sacrifice, the Lord has blessed me.

John—There are people at your school—or maybe even in your ward—who don't want to be there because people treat them poorly. Reach out to them. You can make their lives better. Focusing less on yourself and more on reaching out to others—including family members—will help you discover who you really are.

You know how to invite the Spirit into your life. It means reading your scriptures and praying sincerely, and it might mean doing those things with more effort than you normally do. Instead of just reading a couple of verses, seriously study the scriptures. Instead of just "saying a prayer," pray with real intent. As you do these things, you will feel the Spirit, and the Spirit will help you see things as they really are.

As Mollie began to discover who she really was, she made significant changes in her life. Her life began spiraling upward. Of course things were hard at times, but she kept on going. She began to feel God's love, and that helped her to love herself. Today she is a happy and confident college student, and she was recently married in the temple. You might never know from talking to her that she had been a teenager who felt so awkward. Have you begun to discover who you really are?

Elder Richard G. Scott has reminded us:

> You are of the finest generation that has come to earth. You have prepared yourself well in the premortal existence and have been selected to come forth in this singularly important time in the unfolding of Father in Heaven's plan. . . . The majority of you do not have the slightest idea of how truly capable, noble, and wonderful you are.[9]

- God loves you. You don't have to compare yourself to others. Worry less about what others think about you and instead just reach out to help others.

Be Ye Doers of the Word

- Take the challenge from Sister Tanner's mother. The next time you go out to a dance or other social activity, do everything you can to make your appearance pleasing, but the moment you walk out the door, focus your attention on helping others feel good about themselves. This will help you discover who you really are.

THOUGHTS:

_____
_____
_____
_____
_____

Bonus Scripture:

"I the Lord thy God will hold thy ... hand."

—Isaiah 41:13

Notes

1. Richard G. Scott, "Realize Your Full Potential," *Ensign*, November 2003, 41.
2. Sheri Dew, "Knowing Who You Are—and Who You Have Always Been," BYU Women's Conference, 2001; http://ce.byu.edu/cw/womensconference/archive/2001/dew_sheri.html; accessed 15 February 2011.
3. Jeffrey R. Holland, "To Young Women," *Ensign*, November 2005, 29.
4. Susan W. Tanner, "The Sanctity of the Body," *Ensign*, November 2005, 14.
5. Shaunti Feldhahn and Lisa A. Rice, *For Young Women Only: What You Need to Know about How Guys Think* (Colorado Springs, CO: Multnomah Books, 2006), 121.
6. Hilary Weeks, in Time Out for Women presentations.
7. Tanner, "The Sanctity of the Body," 15.
8. Richard G. Scott, "The Fruits of Obedience," *Brigham Young University 1989–90 Devotional and Fireside Speeches* (Provo: Brigham Young University, 1990), 134.
9. Richard G. Scott, "Do What Is Right," *Brigham Young University 1995–96 Speeches* (Provo: Brigham Young University, 1996), 167.

Chapter 3

Four Things You Should Know about Boys

JOHN — We've talked about some things you need to know about you—especially about who you really are. Now let's talk about some things you should know about boys. Let's face it: For a lot of young women, guys are a major influence in their lives. It can be helpful to understand the other gender a bit better.

We did some research and asked people what they thought young women should know about young men. We asked a lot of people—seminary students, missionaries, young adults, and even the checkout guy at Costco! One thing that was interesting was that across the board, the number one response we received was . . .

funny conversation!

#1: Stay Away

That's right, "Stay away." Kind of funny, huh?

Now, we know that not all young men are bad. I think the comment to "stay away" is reflective of the fact that oftentimes young women connect a lot of their self-worth to the opinions of guys. And that is definitely something to stay away from.

For example, I know one young woman who couldn't wait to turn sixteen. She was so excited to start dating. But nobody called her during her first week of being sixteen. And nobody called the second week. In fact, she didn't get asked on a date that whole year. For her, it was a painful experience.

But I knew another young woman. Guys didn't ask her out either, but for some reason she didn't let it bother her. She was active in sports and school activities. She focused on her family. She didn't "stay away" from guys in the sense of avoiding them like they had cooties, but she did stay away from basing her sense of self-worth on whether or not they paid attention to her.

Lani—John's trying to be nice by saying "I knew another young woman . . . ," but he's talking about me! I went on only one or two dates in high school, and I didn't even get asked to Junior Prom. But I didn't let it bother me! Looking back, I think it was one of the biggest blessings in my life that I did not really date in high school. I found that I did not need attention and approval from guys to feel confident and happy. The roller coaster of emotions that I saw friends ride as they played the "he loves me, he loves me not" game brought such sadness to many. Of course it is fine to date in high school, but remember—don't base your feelings of self-worth on what guys think of you.

[Margin note: Go look up D&C 121:45 to see the key for confidence. ↓ x+y = confidence]

#2: Understand the Great Influence You Can Have on Guys

John—It is amazing what young men will do to impress young women. You have an incredible effect on them. Use this power for good! One young man said, "Girls have no idea of the power they have over us."

Another young man said, "I was doing some stuff that wasn't very good. Then I met a girl who was so good that just being around her made me want to be a better person. She never told me that I needed to make changes, but I made tons of changes just because of who she was."

Young women—you have a powerful influence on others. One member

What Girls Need to Know about Guys

of the Quorum of the Twelve even said that he might not have served a mission if it hadn't been for the encouragement of a young woman.[1]

Think of your power, ladies! There are many ways you can influence young men besides encouraging them to go on missions. You can compliment them when they behave well and encourage them to earn their Duty to God or Eagle Scout awards. You can tell them how much it means to you when they honor their priesthood or do what is right. What a difference you can make!

In one seminary class I asked young men, "When was the last time that a young woman thanked you for being worthy to pass the sacrament?"

Every young man agreed that the answer was "Never!" A couple of them said that older women in the ward had thanked them, but never a younger woman. You could have a great influence on guys just by saying, "Thanks for being worthy."

Lani—As we visited with young men, it was tender to see how much they valued your opinion, and how much they cared about what you thought of them or their behavior. Girls will often tell us to tell the guys to be kinder with their words, but the truth is: guys have feelings too! They can be built up or torn down so easily by what a girl says. What you say has far more weight than what their guy friends say, or maybe even their parents.

★ You can say things like:

"I am so grateful for what you do to honor the priesthood."

"I love it when guys are kind to their mom and sisters. That is really important to me."

"I will marry only a returned missionary."

"I love seeing people who are as honest as you are—that is a rare trait to find these days."

"The sacrament has become so important to me. Thank you for being willing and worthy to administer it."

SERIOUSLY! DO THIS! →

Ladies, you have been given power from God to be an influence on men. Find something you can do today to build up and encourage His sons. Now go do it.

#3: Know What the Guy's Intentions Are

JOHN — This was the idea from the guy at Costco. Though it is sad to admit, some guys have bad motives. Dating a cute guy can be fun, but if his intentions aren't right, you should get away! Consider this story told by a young man named Peter. Notice what his true intentions were.

> The summer after I graduated from high school, there were two girls that I had crushes on. I was going out with both of them from time to time. Things were really serious with one; in fact, she was kind of my girlfriend.
>
> But when she went to college, I wanted to get more serious with the second girl, Amy. I really wanted to kiss her before I went to college. So I made a special plan. I asked a friend to buy some flowers and hide them in the forest. My plan was to take Amy on a romantic walk through the forest, "find" the flowers, and the mood would be set for romance.
>
> Things didn't exactly turn out the way I planned. As Amy and I were walking through the forest, I noticed that somebody was following us. It was deserted, and there shouldn't have been anyone else there. At first I thought it might be my friend hiding the

Are you following this story? This is a guy who admits he is basically toying with the hearts of two young women. His motive has nothing to do with being kind or building up these individuals. He's just trying to steal a kiss!

flowers, but then I started to worry that it was a robber and we were going to get attacked or something.

Either way, I was uncomfortable. Plus, I was beginning to realize that I was being a huge, selfish jerk. We got to the spot and found the flowers, but by this time, any romantic feelings had left me. So we just went home.

Lani — Now we can all be glad that by the end of the story Peter recognized that he was being selfish. But not all guys figure it out.

You should be aware that guys and girls often view hugging, kissing, and other acts of physical affection in different ways. To a girl, a kiss might mean, "I really care about you." To a guy, it could simply mean, "This feels good. I'd like to do more of this."

John — A young lady was at a party when a young man she didn't really know came up to her and said, "Can I kiss you?"

"No!" she said.

"Fine, be that way," the young man said rudely. Although the young man was rude, the young lady was happy. By the boy's actions, she had discovered what his intentions were, and she was doubly glad she had stuck up for what she felt was right.

If a boy is pressuring you to do something that you don't feel good about, that's a pretty good sign that his intentions aren't good. Your parents can also be very good resources to help you determine what a guy's true intentions are. Young women, be careful—if you are going to spend any amount of time with a young man, know what his expectations are!

By the way—we're not telling you that you need to read the flipover part of this book that is for boys, but you might be interested to know that chapter 2 talks about the four different types of boys. That's important for knowing what their intentions are!

#4: Don't Take Every Comment Seriously

JOHN — When we ask young men what they think young women should know about them, they often say, "Tell them not to take everything so seriously. Sometimes we're just joking around."

Interestingly enough, when we ask young women what guys should know about them, they frequently say, "Tell the guys not to put us down or make rude comments, even if they are joking."

This is clearly an important point.

It's easy to get upset when guys say something rude. But let's face it—it's going to happen. We love these words from President Gordon B. Hinckley: "Respect yourself. Do not feel sorry for yourself. Do not dwell on unkind things others may say about you. Particularly, pay no attention to what some boy might say to demean you."[2]

LANI — I love this counsel because I remember myself as a Beehive, completely soaking my pillow with tears because of what "some boy" had said about me, and it happened again for something "some boy" had NOT said about me—can you relate? The instances I am referring to happened most often with my own brothers. But President Hinckley said to pay NO attention. The only way I know how to "pay no attention" is to remember the respect and love Heavenly Father has for me—to respect myself so much that I let negative comments just slide right off me. When I pray and ask to feel the love Heavenly Father has for me, security and confidence surround me, and then it doesn't matter so much what some boy says or does not say.

JOHN — Of course, there are lots of other things to know about guys. We picked these four, hoping that they would help you make sure that you don't allow guys to take away your feelings of divine worth. Remember—you are a daughter of God. You have great worth, no matter what boys say or do!

Bonus Scripture:

"Who knoweth whether thou art come to the kingdom for such a time as this?"

—Esther 4:14

When it comes to guys...
#1: Stay Away (at least until you are the right age)
#2: Understand the Great Influence You Can Have on Guys
#3: Know What the Guy's Intentions Are
#4: Don't Take Every Comment Seriously

Be Ye Doers of the Word

- Use your influence on boys to encourage them to be righteous. Find something specific you could say (like, "Thank you for being worthy to bless the sacrament") that will lift up a young man that you know.

- Remember that boys will often rise to the expectations you have. Think about what expectations you can or should have for a young man.

- Choose another section of this chapter that will help you and then act on it.

1. Richard G. Scott, "Now Is the Time to Serve a Mission," *Ensign*, May 2006, 89.
2. Gordon B. Hinckley, "How Can I Become the Woman of Whom I Dream?" *New Era*, November 2001, 8.

Chapter 4

A Topic You Might Not Want to Hear About

JOHN—There is a topic that is frequently discussed (especially among young women), and originally we weren't going to write about it in this book. But we heard about it so much from the guys we talked to that we felt we needed to include it.

Lani— In fact, as I asked individual guys what they thought girls needed to know about what guys wanted, this was by far the most common topic they mentioned. It was usually the thing they blurted out first, and then when I pushed for more of their thoughts, they would think for a moment and come up with different suggestions. I was amazed that, across the board, this was the number one, first thought. You've probably already guessed what it is.

Yep. Immodesty.

JOHN—The guys said most frequently, "Please tell them we want them to dress modestly."

Prophets have taught us about immodesty. This quote was given in general conference: "Never, I say within the period of my life and experience have I seen such obscene, uncleanly, impure, and suggestive fashions of women's dress as I see today. Some of them are abominable. I lift my voice against these audacious practices and these infamous fashions."[1]

What *Girls* Need to Know about *Guys*

That sounds like it could have been given in the most recent general conference, doesn't it? It was actually President Joseph F. Smith speaking in 1913! Immodesty is a problem that has been around for a while.

Lani — If you're like the average young woman, you might have a hard time understanding *why* immodesty is such a big deal, or you may think that you have already mastered this. We know that our bodies are sacred temples and that we should keep them covered. We know that when we dress modestly, we are showing respect for ourselves. We are reverencing womanhood. President Thomas S. Monson simply said, "When you dress modestly, you show respect for your Heavenly Father and for yourself."²

So respecting yourself is one reason to dress modestly; however, the young men talked to us about another reason why it's important for young women to dress modestly. Putting it bluntly, one young man said, "I try really hard to have the Spirit with me, and when I see all these girls in school showing cleavage and underwear, it makes it really hard to feel the Spirit. I don't want to see that!"

For some girls, this statement will be hard to understand. It's important that you know that guys are VISUAL. What guys *see* has a huge effect on them. Let's use an analogy.

> "Don't read this. No, really, don't read it. Just look at the letters, and don't read the words. Impossible, isn't it? There is no way to just notice the letters without reading the word. That's what it's like for a guy."³ When girls are dressed immodestly, if guys aren't careful, they will automatically start having inappropriate thoughts.

STOP reading this!

JOHN— Of course, guys are responsible for controlling their eyes, but notice what Elder Dallin H. Oaks taught. Speaking directly to young women he said, "Please understand that if you dress immodestly, you are magnifying [the problem of pornography] by becoming pornography to some of the men who see you."[4]

What happens to you when you look at this?

LANI—I used to think that it was the guys' responsibility to control their eyes and to control their thoughts. And, to some extent, it is. But then I read about a high school teacher who had some female students who complained about the dress codes imposed on them. The girls said the guys shouldn't be such "perverts" for thinking those things anyway. So the teacher brought in some fancy chocolates the next day and put them out on a table in front of the class. He went on with the class as usual. After a while, he asked the class, "Who has looked at those chocolates more than one time? Who wants some of those chocolates?" Everyone raised their hand. He then said, "Too bad, no one gets chocolates today. Ladies, that is how it is for guys when you dress to bring attention to your body."[5]

It helps me to remember that God made men this way, and He called what He made good. He wants men to be attracted to women. Men are not evil for having that desire God gave them. But He also told them not to linger or lust. How would you like to have chocolate all around you all day and be told you can't look or partake? With all the immodesty the world shows today, it seems like an exhausting chore for a righteous young man to always feel the need to turn away or change his thoughts.

What *Girls* Need to Know about *Guys*

JOHN—An author named Joshua Harris put it this way. Speaking to young women, he wrote:

> You may not realize this, but we guys most commonly struggle with our eyes. I think many girls are innocently unaware of the difficulty a guy has in remaining pure when looking at a girl who is dressed immodestly. Now I don't want to dictate your wardrobe, but, honestly speaking, I would be blessed if girls considered more than fashion when shopping for clothes. Yes, guys are responsible for maintaining self-control, but you can help by refusing to wear clothing designed to attract attention to your body.... I know many girls who would look great in shorter skirts or tighter blouses, and they know it. But they choose to dress modestly. They take the responsibility of guarding their brothers' eyes. To these women and others like them, I'm grateful.[6]

Lani—I think it might be helpful to hear from a woman's perspective. Here's part of a talk that was given by Susan Bednar, wife of Elder David A. Bednar. She was speaking to college-age girls at BYU–Idaho. Pay close attention to what she has to say.

> Let me tell you of an embarrassing experience I had when I was your age.... I was wearing a tight [shirt] similar to most of the ... tight shirts I see you young women wearing. I'd gone into the ... store to buy something to eat, when I heard two sleazy boys make some extremely vulgar comments about me.... I felt violated by their comments; I felt dirty and cheap. Inside I just wanted to say, "I'm not that kind of a girl." But the top I was wearing didn't reflect that. I never wore that top or

SAD!

anything tight like it again. I want to warn you, many of you are sending the wrong message about who you are by the tight tops you wear."[7]

Lani—You might think that Sister Bednar's case was one-of-a-kind and that most guys wouldn't think or talk like that. Let me tell you something—many of them do. I think that some young women simply don't understand the ways that immodesty influences guys. Sister Bednar continues:

> Let me share an experience I had not long ago at the minor league baseball field in Idaho Falls. Our family was sitting in the grandstands at the baseball field when a group of men who had been drinking came and sat in front of us. Not long after these men sat down, two pretty young girls with cute figures wearing tight tops and short shorts walked in front of the grandstands not far from where these men were sitting. I listened to these vulgar men verbally and visually undress these young women in their minds as these girls walked by. It was disgusting. . . . What was hard for me about this situation is that these young women . . . looked just as innocent as you girls look, and they weren't dressed any different than I see many of you dress when you are in your apartments and off campus. . . .
>
> You can't believe all the female students I've walked past who were sitting in a chair, and when I looked down I could see their bikini underpants or even worse. I think you know what I mean. I'm sorry to be so blunt. I'm just telling you what I saw. When I looked into the faces of these girls, I could tell they probably weren't even aware of what they were showing. But young women, for the

sake of the priesthood holders . . . you cannot continue to be unaware.[8]

JOHN— The boys have talked to us about how much they want you to dress modestly so that they can have the Spirit with them. And that is important. Keep in mind, though, that modesty is a blessing for *you* too. In fact, in a radio interview, as Elder and Sister Bednar were discussing Sister Bednar's talk we've just quoted from, they both emphasized that the message was not about modesty, it was about reverencing womanhood.

Sometimes it is really hard to dress modestly. We know that. But often the hardest things are the most important. And it's not just hard in the United States. At an Especially for Youth program we met Eleni, a young woman from Guatemala. She shared the following story with us:

> I go to a private school, and we all have to wear uniforms. Part of the uniform is a black skirt. Everyone wears really short skirts, but I always wear a more modest skirt. When the day came to have our class picture taken for the yearbook,

Is It Too . . . ?

So, you try something on, and you think "Is this too _____?" (Fill in the blank) Too low? Too tight? Too short? Too revealing? Too sexy?

I found that a good rule of thumb is this: If I am asking the question, then it usually IS too_____. It works for fashion too—is it too old-school? Too striped? Too wrinkled? Sorry to say, but if you have to ask, it probably is.

> "A guy will have a tendency to treat you like you are dressed. If you are dressed like a flesh buffet, don't be surprised when he treats you like a piece of meat."[9]

everybody wanted me to wear an immodest skirt because we all had to match. I would not wear that skirt, so everybody had to wear a longer skirt that day. All of the girls were mad at me, but I stood firm. It was hard, but it was worth it.

Eleni is not alone. We know you and many others are standing strong by dressing modestly. Sister Carol B. Thomas, then of the Young Women general presidency, shared this example of a young woman who was blessed by dressing modestly. She said:

> One of the hardest things for many of you is modesty. How can we apply the spiritual power of our baptism to the principle of modesty? We hope one of the things that makes you different from the world is the way you dress. Marcie Matthews, a Laurel from Chicago, Illinois, shares her story:
>
> "Recently we had a Mutual activity on the importance of modesty. Every lesson before I felt like I was a modest dresser, but I knew there was still something I could change—my shorts and the length of my skirts . . . [and] I had bought [them] with my own money. . . . I went home wanting to go straight to my closet and throw away everything that was not modest so it wouldn't be there to tempt me. . . .
>
> "It was hard for me to part with my favorite skirts and the shorts that I loved so much, but I did. You will never see me in short shorts or short skirts again.
>
> "I have never felt better about myself. I love being able to walk into the temple and church and feel like I am a child of God and am representing Him . . . by the clothes that I wear."
>
> Marcie's great example epitomizes our Young Women theme. You know, the part that says, "We stand

as witnesses of God at all times and in all things"—and <u>in all prom dresses</u>.¹⁰

Lani — You can be modest, ladies! The young men really want you to be. Being modest will bless you—and them.

- It can be hard to be modest—but you can do it! Guys <u>really</u> want you to be modest!

Be Ye Doers of the Word

- Get together with your mom, or, if you are really serious, your brother, and go through your clothes to see how modest they really are. If you're in doubt as to whether something is modest, get rid of it, and this does <u>not</u> mean stuffing it in the back of your closet!

Notes

1. Joseph F. Smith, Conference Report, October 1913, 7.
2. Thomas S. Monson, "Be Thou an Example," *Ensign*, May 2005, 115.
3. Shaunti Feldhahn and Lisa A. Rice, *For Young Women Only: What You Need to Know about How Guys Think* (Colorado Springs, CO: Multnomah Books, 2006), 100.
4. Dallin H. Oaks, "Pornography," *Ensign*, May 2005, 90.
5. Feldhahn, *For Young Women Only*, 106, 107.
6. Joshua Harris, *I Kissed Dating Goodbye* (Sisters, OR: Multnomah Publishers, 1997), 99.
7. Susan Bednar, "Reverencing Womanhood," Brigham Young University–Idaho, six-stake fireside, 16 September 2001; http://www.byui.edu/Presentations/Transcripts/MiscellaneousAddresses/2001_09_16_Bednarsusan.htm; accessed 21 December 2010.
8. Ibid.
9. Justin Lookadoo and Hayley DiMarco, *Dateable: Are You? Are They?* (Grand Rapids, MI: Fleming H. Revell, 2003), 118.
10. Carol B. Thomas, "Spiritual Power of Our Baptism," *Ensign*, May 1999, 93.

THOUGHTS: _____
_____
_____
_____
_____
_____
_____
_____
_____
_____

Chapter 5

Expect (and Accept) the Respect

Lani — Okay, ladies, I am going to share with you some experiences from my life. Get ready for some juicy details. Picture John and me on our first date. As we walked from my house to the car, he opened the door for me, of course. That is the easiest part because the guy is usually walking with the girl to the car, and it takes only a little foresight to have his hand reach the door handle before hers. We had a pleasant conversation during the car ride.

When we arrived at his apartment, he got out of the car, and it looked like he was coming around to open my door, so I sat and waited. But then someone from an upper floor of his apartment building yelled to him, and the two of them started talking. So there I sat, unsure of what to do, while John was talking. I did not know the person he was talking to, and I hardly knew John. Was he the kind of guy who would open my door or not?

This is key! <u>I decided to wait.</u> Well, it was a very long ten seconds, but John did finish talking and kindly opened my door. That's the first lesson from this story—expect the respect. Plan on the guy doing the chivalrous thing. I later found out that John was the kind of guy who always opened the door for a lady. I was grateful that I had expected John to demonstrate respect for me by opening the door, and he did it all throughout our courtship, and even after we were married. It added something beautiful to our relationship. Remember this phrase—"Expect the Respect."

After we had been married about a year and a half, things were very busy with a new little baby. I often was eager to get the baby out of the car seat at the end of a car ride, or I had something I needed to do quickly. Waiting for John to open my door before or after getting into the car seemed more of a hassle and sometimes even inconvenient. I even thought about how many seconds of my life I was wasting sitting in the car waiting. Ten seconds a day times seven days a week equals more than a minute each week, so in a year I would waste an hour of my life . . . plus my baby was waiting, which doubled the problem, of course. Sounds like silly thinking, but I ended up telling John that I knew he loved me and respected me but he did not need to open the car door for me anymore.

He simply said, "Okay," and that was the end of it.

> When you really know you are a daughter of God and you really feel it, it affects how you act. True doctrine changes behavior. It will not only affect how you fix yourself up, how you dress, how you interact with others, but it will affect how you expect to be treated by others. Think of a princess in ancient times. If she were taken out of her castle, she would still expect to be treated like a princess. There were certain things she would not put up with. This is one reason we really need to internalize the principles from the first chapters because if we REALLY feel we are God's supreme creation, we will expect to be treated respectfully.

But it did not take long before I started to feel a difference. So I said, "John, I would really like it if you would start opening my door again."

And he did.

Now here is the second lesson from this story: Accept the respect. A few years later (after many doors had been opened for me), we were living in Miami, Florida. When we pulled into the driveway after a family activity visiting the Everglades, John turned off the car and opened his door so that he could come and get mine. Immediately our son, Levi (who was four at the time), yelled excitedly, "Wait, Dad! I want to get Mom's door."

Quick as a flash, he unbuckled his seatbelt in the back of the minivan and proceeded to climb over his sisters in the next row. Then he climbed onto my lap and opened my door from the inside of the car while sitting on my lap in the passenger seat. My heart melted! I gave him a big kiss! I saw that by accepting John's respect, we were teaching our son a valuable lesson about honoring women. I was grateful I had chosen to accept the respect that had been offered to me over the years.

JOHN — I love these principles that Lani teaches—expect the respect and accept the respect. Let's discuss them a little more.

Expect the Respect

Suppose you are walking into a building with a young man. You are about one step closer to the door than he is. Should you open the door or wait for him to do it? It can be an awkward situation—you don't want him to think that you don't know how to open a door!

Don't worry about that—simply expect the respect. Most guys want to have opportunities to honor women. If he thinks you're a dork because you expect guys to show common courtesy, he's probably not a guy you want to get attached to anyway.

DO IT!

LANI — How do you go about expecting the respect? It's easy—just expect the guy to do the appropriate thing. When you come to a door, let him open it. Wait for him to come around and open your car door. If you're

What If He Doesn't Open the Door?

Justin, an eighteen-year-old young man, was getting ready to go to a stake dance when he received a phone call from a woman in his ward. She was wondering if he could pick up her fourteen-year-old daughter and take her to the dance. He agreed and picked her up.

They arrived at the church building, and Justin began walking toward the church. He was all the way to the front door of the stake center when he realized that the young woman wasn't with him. He walked back to the car and, sure enough, there she was, waiting for him to open the door. Now that's what we call expecting the respect!

Once when I told that story, a lady came up to me and said that when she was in high school a guy had asked her to go to a movie with him. When they arrived at the theater, the young man went into the theater, bought tickets, bought popcorn, and sat down in the movie, all before he realized that she was still in the car waiting for him to open the door. Ouch. We think that was their last date.

You don't have to go to the extreme of waiting forever. If a young man is not giving you the respect you deserve, be as gracious as you can be. Some guys aren't used to doing these simple courtesies for women. They may not have been taught this principle in their home. If you want to bless him for the rest of his life, kindly say something like, "I really like it when guys open doors for me," or even more specifically, "I would really like it if you opened the door for me." And even if he doesn't listen to you, don't let that stop you from continuing to expect the respect in the future! Guys are simpler than we think. Often they just need to be taught or clearly told, and then they are happy to comply!

at a restaurant and he pulls out a chair, assume that he is pulling it out for you and not for himself. (Be sure to smile and sincerely say "thank you!" as you sit down. Even if he didn't intend to pull out the chair for you, he'll be glad to get credit for it—and he'll remember the next time.)

JOHN— Here's a tip: When a guy does something courteous for you, be extra gracious and let him know you appreciate it. Encourage him. And, when appropriate, wait for him. If you're driving together and he has gotten out of the car, and you're wondering if he's going to get your door, don't be afraid to count to ten slowly and silently before even thinking about opening your door. Fiddle around with your purse, pretend you lost something under the seat, do anything to stall for time . . . guys will eventually figure it out.

Part of expecting to be respected is clearly communicating to the guy what it is you want. Our friend Chrislyn was in her twenties and was dating a returned missionary named Ryan. They were on their second date, and she could tell that he was going to kiss her. She thought about her feelings and what she really wanted and said, "Let's wait. I don't want to wreck a good thing." Later Chrislyn said, "He was really respectful of that, and I felt good that we hadn't kissed. I needed him to show me that I could trust him before I started sharing that part of myself with him. That was one of the best decisions we ever made for our relationship." Chrislyn and Ryan eventually married in the temple; Chrislyn said that their relationship was wonderful from the beginning because she had the courage to *expect* Ryan to respect her wishes (and kudos to Ryan for respecting them!).

But what if a guy still doesn't respect you, even if you make it clear you want to be respected? It's simple—stay away from that guy! Sadly, some young women feel that they don't deserve to be respected. We talked once with a girl we'll call Liz. She was struggling with depression and, due to some tough family circumstances, wasn't feeling much love from her parents. She wrote, "I have had the same boyfriend for almost ten months. . . . He is really fun to hang out with because he has a fun personality. But within the first few months of our relationship something didn't feel quite right. He didn't respect me as much as he should. He says rude things to me about the way I look, and he will never go to the movie of my choice. I think the reason we are still together is because I don't want to be alone with all the hard things going on in my life right now." Her boyfriend also made fun of her for going to youth conference. He told her that if he got drunk and cheated on her while she was gone, it was her fault for leaving for youth conference.

A turning point for Liz came when she understood this quote from Elder Jeffrey R. Holland. He said, "In a dating and courtship relationship, I would not have you spend five minutes with someone who belittles you, one who is constantly critical of you, one who is cruel at your expense and may even call it humor. Life is tough enough without the person who is supposed to love you leading the assault on your self-esteem, your sense of dignity, your confidence, and your joy. In this person's care, you deserve to feel physically safe and emotionally secure."[2]

> Respect yourself. . . . Never forget that you came to earth as a child of the divine Father, with something of divinity in your very makeup.[1]
> —President Gordon B. Hinckley

Liz realized that she did not deserve to be treated so poorly. She determined that she would walk away from her boyfriend because he was not giving her the respect that she deserved. Listen, girls—if you are in an abusive relationship, get out and get help! You deserve to be honored and respected. And if you have a friend in an abusive relationship, help your friend get out and get help!

John Hilton III and Lani Hilton

Accept the Respect

JOHN—Lani already talked about one reason why you should accept the respect—it creates habits that may even bless your children.

But accepting the respect will also immediately bless the young men who are honoring you! When a young man shows simple courtesies to a young woman, he will feel good inside because he is doing something good. He will feel the Spirit. Even if you really would rather open your own door, let the boy do it. You will be helping him feel the Spirit of the Lord.

Lani—The duties of a teacher in the Aaronic Priesthood are outlined in the Doctrine and Covenants. Part of these duties is to watch over and strengthen the Church (see D&C 20:53). Brother David L. Beck, the Young Men general president, once said that this definitely includes watching over the young women.[3] So, by accepting the respect they give, you are <u>helping them honor and fulfill their priesthood duties</u>. That is an important reason to do it!

You can help!

JOHN—Another reason you should accept respect from young men (even if it is awkwardly given) is that it will encourage young men to respect other young women.

I spoke once with a young man who had tried to open the door for a young woman. She had rudely said, "I can open my own door." He now is afraid to try to open the door for other women. Because one young woman did not accept the respect, she made it less likely that other young women will receive the respect they deserve.

On another occasion, I noticed a mother with two teenage children walking into a store. The mother and daughter were a few steps ahead of the son, but they waited for the son to catch up and open the door for them. Now this was one of those double doors, where you walk in one door, and then five feet later there is another door. Sometimes those can be tricky—should you open the second door to reciprocate?

Nope! The mother and sister waited again for the son to open the second door. Their willingness to go a bit slower and accept the respect he offered them was providing valuable training for this young man. When you expect and accept the respect you deserve, you are helping to shape the young men around you into the kind of men they need to be—men who honor and reverence womanhood.

Another part of accepting the respect is to graciously accept compliments when they are given to you. How do you think a young man would feel in the following conversation?

Young man: "You look pretty tonight."
Young woman: "No, I don't."
Young man: "No, really, you do."
Young woman: "No, I'm ugly."
Young man: "Uh . . ."

You can see that this puts him in an awkward situation. When somebody compliments you, simply say, "Thank you."

Lani — When a young man offers you respect, accept it! It may be inconvenient or a little awkward, but do it anyway! If there aren't enough chairs at the table or in the room and he offers you his chair, accept it! Help strengthen that young man in his ability to honor women.

We once had a really special experience when we were asked to pick up a General Authority from the airport and take him to a young single adult fireside. The spirit that was present in the car and when he spoke was undeniable. I knew he was a servant of God. The whole time he made me feel so honored to be a woman. We were in a small car, and it seemed very appropriate for him to have the leg room of the front seat. When I offered him the front seat, he refused and gave it to me. He said, "I would never separate a man from his wife." As we traveled, he was so gracious and kind and poured on the compliments.

JOHN—We had known that we would spend time with him, so we had prepared some questions to ask him. I was so focused on the questions we wanted to ask and in getting his wisdom that I completely forgot to give him the dinner that we had brought with us (it was in the trunk of my car). When we arrived at the stake center, I realized what I had done. . . . I couldn't believe it! My one chance to feed a member of the Quorum of the Twelve dinner and I had blown it! I jumped out of the car and began rummaging through the trunk trying to find his dinner. Meanwhile, the General Authority got out of the car and opened the door for Lani!

Lani—Even though we had arrived later than planned, he didn't rush ahead of me as we walked to the chapel. He just talked with me personally and always waited for me to go through the door first. When I was with him, I felt like I was in the presence of <u>somebody who truly honored womanhood</u>. *Amazing experience*

    Girls, a real man will honor you. Expect the respect you deserve as a daughter of a Heavenly King. Graciously and gratefully accept the respect that is offered.

Bonus Scripture:

"And charity . . . is kind."
—Moroni 7:45

- Expect the respect!
- Accept the respect!

Be Ye Doers of the Word

- Think about what it means for you to expect the respect.
- What situation will you find yourself in today where you could apply this?

THOUGHTS:
_____
_____
_____
_____
_____
_____
_____
_____
_____
_____
_____

Notes

1. Gordon B. Hinckley, "How Can I Become the Woman of Whom I Dream?" *New Era*, November 2001, 8.
2. Jeffrey R. Holland, "How Do I Love Thee?" Brigham Young University devotional speech, 15 February 2000, 4; http://speeches.byu.edu/reader/reader.php?id=1618&x=59&y=7; accessed 21 December 2010.
3. David L. Beck, "Dating and Virtue," *Ensign*, September 2010, 18.

Chapter 6

What about Kissing?

JOHN— "Is kissing okay?" This is a question that many teenagers want answered. And in a book about what girls should know about guys, this is definitely an important topic. Although we could write an entire book just on this subject, we want to focus on a few key questions in this chapter.

Why Is It So Important to Stay Morally Clean?

Why? Why? Why?

There are so many good reasons why we should stay morally clean. Consider these two doctrinal reasons: First, our bodies are sacred gifts from God (see 1 Corinthians 6:19–20); therefore, we should only do things with our bodies that God approves of. Second, having sexual relationships outside of marriage makes a mockery of the Atonement. Elder Jeffrey R. Holland taught that having sexual relations outside of marriage "desecrates the Atonement of Christ. . . . And when one mocks the Son of Righteousness, one steps into a realm of heat hotter and holier than the noonday sun. You cannot do so and not be burned."[1] Take a minute and reread those sentences—can you feel the seriousness of violating the law of chastity?

In addition to these doctrinal reasons for staying morally clean, consider these other important

We don't expect you to read everything we wrote to the guys on their side of the book, but we do recommend you read at least the chapter "What about Kissing?" It has some important information we didn't include in this chapter.

reasons that we sometimes might not think about. First, keeping the law of chastity strengthens society. Sister Sheri Dew said (and note her emphasis), "*The single most pervasive threat to the stability and future of the family is sexual immorality in all its forms.* Nothing would do more to strengthen the families of the world than a resurgence of moral virtue, particularly sexual purity."[2] Think of that! Nothing will strengthen the families of the world more than society returning to virtue.

Another important reason why you should stay morally clean is to strengthen the family you will have one day. *For the Strength of Youth* says, "When you obey God's commandment to be sexually pure . . . you prepare yourself to build a strong marriage and to bring children into the world as part of a loving family."[3] As one young man said, "I am keeping myself clean, and I hope to find a girl who is doing the same thing. That will help us have a strong foundation together in our marriage." The First Presidency (in 1942!) said, "Sexual purity is youth's most precious possession."[4] When you save this most precious possession for your eternal companion, you strengthen your future marriage.

There are many other reasons that we could mention as to *why* it's so important to stay morally clean, but we will highlight just one more. To put it simply, losing your virtue will hurt you emotionally.

A study of 6,500 adolescents showed that sexually active young women were three times more likely to have depression than abstinent girls were, and that sexually active young men were twice as likely to be depressed. Sexually active young women were three times more likely than their chaste counterparts to commit suicide; sexually active young men were eight times more likely than chaste young men to commit suicide. The vast majority of sexually active teenagers wish that they had saved their virtue.[5]

Recent research has shown that "Casual sex . . . rewires the brain and desensitizes a person (male or female) to the brain chemicals that promote connection and intimacy."[6] Over time, if people have sexual encounters with multiple partners, the bonding substance that the brain produces when sexual intimacy occurs loses its power. These researchers found that even encounters such as passionate kissing (making out) could trigger chemical responses in the brain that would lead to emotional damage. Yikes! They found our brains are wired to create bonds with those whom we have intimate physical relationships with. If we are casual with these relationships, it becomes more difficult to form meaningful bonds.⁷

Lani—Although this brain research is fairly recent, it should not come as a surprise to us. *For the Strength of Youth* says, "When you obey God's commandment to be sexually pure . . . you protect yourself from the emotional damage that *always* comes from sharing physical intimacies with someone outside of marriage."⁸ Check that out. It is not occasionally or sometimes. It is always. THERE WILL ALWAYS BE EMOTIONAL DAMAGE from sharing physical intimacies outside of marriage. Always. Please, please understand—you will feel better about yourself and be more emotionally whole as you stay morally clean.

Do Guys and Girls View Kissing Differently?

John—That would be a big YES. To a young woman, a kiss is often a sign of affection that means "I really like you." To a guy, a kiss usually means "This feels good. I want more." As one young man bluntly said, "Girls think, 'he's kissing me because he loves me,' whereas in reality, he's usually not."⁹ If you give away your kisses, you may be taking something that is sacred to you and wasting it on a boy who doesn't really even care about you.

What Girls Need to Know about Guys

How Can I Keep from Going Too Far?

Lani — Let's take a look at another question that we often hear: How far can I go and still not sin?

There are at least three ways to answer this question.

Answer #1:

For the Strength of Youth says, "Before marriage, do not do anything to arouse the powerful emotions that must be expressed only in marriage. Do not participate in passionate kissing, lie on top of another person, or touch the private, sacred parts of another person's body, with or without clothing. Do not allow anyone to do that with you."[10]

Notice that the first sentence gives a general guideline. If you are doing something that is arousing emotions that should only be expressed in marriage, you shouldn't be doing it. *For the Strength of Youth* also gives four specific things that we should not participate in:

1. Passionate kissing.
2. Lying on top of another person.
3. Touching the private, sacred parts of another person's body—with or without clothing.
4. Allowing somebody else to touch the private, sacred parts of your body—with or without clothing.

You must absolutely make certain you do not participate in these things!

Answer #2:

John — The question, "How far can I go and still not sin?" *is a terrible question*! That question says, "Okay, there is a line of sin, and I want to go right up to that line but still not cross it." The problem is, the closer you get to the line, the harder it is to stop. President Henry B. Eyring (then a member of the Quorum of the Twelve) said, "The question that really matters is this: 'How can I learn to sense even the beginning of sin and so repent early?'"[11]

So since *For the Strength of Youth* says, "Do not participate in passionate kissing," the question that we need to answer is, "What standard can I set for myself to make sure I never get close to passionate kissing?" It's not about "how far can I go?" but "how can I make sure I don't sin?"

Answer #3:

Lani—Now that we know what the line of sin is, and that we should stay far away from it, what should we do? Elder Richard G. Scott gave this counsel, which we plead with you to follow: "Firmly establish personal standards. Choose a time of deep spiritual reflection, when there is no pressure on you, and you can confirm your decisions by sacred impressions. Decide then what you will do and what you will not do to express feelings. The Spirit will guide you. Then do not vary from those decisions no matter how right it may seem when the temptation comes."[12]

[Key points!]

One of the most important things that you can do to stay morally clean is to prayerfully set a standard that you will never deviate from. There is something powerful that happens when we are keeping a commandment, not because our Young Women leader told us to, or because of what we read in a book, but because the Holy Ghost has told us to do it. That is why we want you to pray about it. We know that you can receive individual guidance from the Spirit. Maybe some of you will feel prompted to say, "From this point on, I will not kiss a boy until after I have graduated from high school." Or you might feel a prompting saying, "I should only do things that I would feel comfortable doing in front of my parents." The important thing is that you pray and have the Holy Ghost confirm those standards to you—and then live them.

We don't know what has happened to you in the past—if there has been sin, you can repent. You can also decide that, from this time *forward, you will be 100 percent clean. We promise you that as you live the law of chastity you will be happy.*

Notes

1. Jeffrey R. Holland, "Personal Purity," *Ensign*, November 1998, 76.
2. Sheri L. Dew, "The Power of Virtue," talk given at World Congress of Families V in Amsterdam, the Netherlands, on 10 August 2009; http://www.ldschurchnews.com/articles/57746/Sheri-L-Dew-The-Power-of-Virtue.html; accessed 21 December 2010.
3. *For the Strength of Youth* (Salt Lake City: The Church of Jesus Christ of Latter-day Saints, 2001), 26.
4. In James R. Clark, comp. *Messages of the First Presidency of The Church of Jesus Christ of Latter-day Saints, 1935–51*, vol. 6 (Salt Lake City: Bookcraft, 1975), 150.
5. Robert Rector, Kirk Johnson, and Lauren Noyes, "Sexually Active Teenagers Are More Likely to Be Depressed and to Attempt Suicide," *The Heritage Foundation*, 3 June 2003; http://www.heritage.org/Research/Reports/2003/06/Sexually-Active-Teenagers-Are-More-Likely-to-Be-Depressed; accessed 21 December 2010.
6. Chris Freeland book review, on Joe McIlhaney and Freda McKissic Bush, *Hooked: New Science on How Casual Sex Is Affecting Our Children*; http://chrisfreeland.blogspot.com/2009/11/hooked-book-review.html; accessed 21 December 2010.
7. See Joe McIlhaney and Freda McKissic Bush, *Hooked: New Science on How Casual Sex Is Affecting Our Children* (Chicago: Northfield Publishing, 2008).
8. *For the Strength of Youth*, 26; emphasis added.
9. Shaunti Feldhahn and Lisa A. Rice, *For Young Women Only: What You Need to Know about How Guys Think* (Colorado Springs, CO: Multnomah Books, 2006), 155.
10. *For the Strength of Youth*, 27.
11. Henry B. Eyring, "Do Not Delay," *Ensign*, November 1999, 34.
12. Richard G. Scott, "Do What Is Right," *Brigham Young University 1995–96 Speeches* (Provo: Brigham Young University, 1996), 173.

- Our bodies are sacred gifts from God.
- Having sexual relationships outside of marriage makes a mockery of the Atonement and can affect your relationships.
- Set firm standards to stay far away from sin.

Be Ye Doers of the Word

- Pray about a specific standard you will set for yourself to keep from ever getting close to the line of sin.
- Think of a friend who needs the information in this chapter. Share it with him or her.

THOUGHTS:
_____
_____
_____
_____
_____
_____

Chapter 7

What Guys Wish Girls Knew

JOHN—So what do guys wish girls knew? We have asked hundreds of LDS young men, and we found some common themes in their responses to this question. Most go along with counsel you have already received from Church leaders and your parents. Here it is—straight from the mouths of the guys themselves!

You Really Are Awesome

"Young women should know how awesome we think they are. They can do something stupid, and it is all good."—Tanner

"Guys like girls who have self-confidence. Don't think so little of yourself that you can't even converse, but it is also not right to have so much confidence that you are snobby."—Jeffrey

"Be aware of wearing too much makeup. Some is good, but you are already so pretty."—Jared

Modest Really Is Hottest

"It is so much easier to talk to a girl when she is modest. I know that some guys are attracted to immodest girls, but they aren't the kind of guys you want to be with. Just like girls aren't impressed with guys who try to show off, we aren't impressed with immodest girls."—Camden

What Girls Need to Know about Guys

"Modesty—I really appreciate it. It is a lot less distracting. I find it easier to talk to a girl who is modest."—Kevin

"The truth is, guys really don't like immodesty." —Matt*

*Plus 78 similar comments (see also chapter 4 on both the guys' and girls' side). WE ARE NOT JOKING!

Be Smart

"Sometimes it seems like girls act dumb because they think guys will like it. Don't say something dumb to impress us and don't act like an airhead. It's really not impressive."—Lucas

Be Grateful and Compliment Us

"Do you like someone to tell you that you look nice or that you did something well? Guys like that too!"—Trevor

Colossians 4:6

"Be appreciative. The only girl I went out with in high school—she asked me—I took to lunch. I paid for her to eat, and she did not eat anything! I was so irritated. Show gratitude for the boy's effort. Be happy and smile all the time. Everyone likes people who are happy."—Adam

"Guys like it when you express gratitude. Show gratitude that they have taken the time to plan an activity or give you their time. If they help you with something, be grateful and say thank you."—Sam

"Compliment us. Some girls respect us for holding the priesthood and for being worthy to perform ordinances they need. I was so happy when a girl told me she appreciated my priesthood efforts and she said thank you."—Tom

Accept Kindness from Us

"Don't fish for compliments and don't deny compliments when we give them. If we say, 'You look nice,' we mean it. You don't need to say, 'No, I don't,' or go around saying, 'I'm so ugly,' or 'I'm so fat.'"—Justin

Some Initiating Is Good, But Not Too Much

"Don't call boys all the time. Don't throw yourself at boys. It sends a message that you're desperate. Don't be in a rush to pair off. It is so rare that the person you date in high school will end up being your husband, so have fun being with a lot of people."—Bryce

"We like it when girls do some initiating. Maybe a call sometime or a text, or you try to be nice. It is nice to not *always* be the one initiating everything. But don't do too much. It gets annoying when girls call all the time or throw themselves at you."—Joe

Be Kind to Us—We Have Feelings Too

"Remember we aren't perfect. We are just doing our best. So look for the good. Don't judge a guy too quickly. Don't be someone who rips on guys to other girls and talks only about the negative. Girls need to be more respectful and appreciative, even if there are things they wish were different. I wish girls would see guys as children of God and then talk about them only that way."—Seth

"The golden rule: Just as it applies to you, it applies to us."—John

"It is very rude for girls to go off—even a few feet—with their girlfriends or their groups and whisper. It's so rude!"—Brian

"Make the person across the table from you (the guy you are on the date with) feel like the coolest guy in the world. You have the opportunity to bless him for the rest of his life by taking the hour you have with him to build him up as a child of God. Be interested in everything about him while you are with him, even if you are not interested romantically."—Aaron

What Girls Need to Know about Guys

Be Honest When Turning Down Dates

"When it is time for courtship, honest open communication is really the best way for breakups. It is much easier for the guy to hear a "no" answer or "let's just be friends" earlier on in the relationship than after you have strung him along."—Alex

"Guys like it when you are honest. Don't keep going on dates just because they ask you if you are really not interested in pursuing anything."—Lars

"I wish girls would speak their mind more and not speak code. It is nice when they say what they think."—Mike

"Don't break dates. Don't say you would love to go and then never be available."—Josh

Be Virtuous

"Guys like girls who are very virtuous—so virtuous that the boy has to strive to be better and rise to a higher spiritual plane. One girl I knew was very spiritual and virtuous, and I knew I wouldn't even have a chance to be with her if I did not improve. She has blessed my life, and she doesn't even know it."—Brandon

"It is a huge turnoff when a guy sees a girl doing something unvirtuous."—Cameron

About Chivalry

"We don't mind being reminded. If we need to be doing something or we forgot about something, let us know. Educate us."—Mitch

"*Never* shut down courtesy. It hurts our feelings. We're just trying to be nice. I have tried to open the door for some girls, and they yell at me, saying they can open their own door. Don't yell at me for trying to be nice."—Ryan

- Guys are pretty easy to understand. If you still aren't sure what they want, go back and read this chapter again!

Be Ye Doers of the Word

- Select one piece of advice given by one of the young men in this chapter and make a plan for what you will do to act on it.

THOUGHTS:
_____
_____
_____
_____
_____
_____
_____
_____
_____
_____

Be Careful around Guys

"Girls should know that teenage boys have only one thing on their minds—and it isn't casual conversation. That is why girls should be so careful about dating boys who don't hold very strong moral values. It is also why they should cover themselves up, according to Church standards, and that includes no bikinis, no bare shoulders, no shorts above the knees—I don't care what your age is. Girls who don't believe this have their heads in the sand and are asking for trouble they could regret the rest of their lives."—Marshall

Help Us Become Better

"There was this girl that I really wanted to get to know, but I knew I needed to be better if she was even going to notice me. So I signed up for seminary and started doing things I knew I needed to be doing. I have really changed for the better, and she has no idea that it was because of her."—Chad

"You don't really have to say a lot—just be a really good example and be as righteous as you can be. There are some girls who inspire me to be my best when I'm around them. Don't be afraid to say to a guy something like, 'I wish you wouldn't talk like that in front of me.' Most guys will listen. If they don't, they're not worth your time anyway."—Levi

Chapter 8

Potential Pitfalls

JOHN — I once gave a talk encouraging young men to respect and honor young women. After the talk, a woman in the audience told me, "I appreciate what you said to the young men, but you let the young women who were in the audience off the hook."

"What do you mean?" I said.

"I'm sure the young women loved hearing you tell the young men to respect them—but there are things they should be doing to honor young men."

Hmmm...

That comment really made me think. Besides the messages that you deserve to be honored, and you should expect and accept the respect, here are a few pitfalls that should be avoided.

Pitfall #1: Being Unkind to Young Men

Lexi was at a school dance with a group of friends. She could tell that Colton had his eye on her—he had been flirting with her all night. The problem was that her best friend had a huge crush on him.

At the end of the night, Colton came up to Lexi and asked, "Can I get your phone number?"

"Sure," said Lexi. Without thinking, she said, "It's 305-444-4getit." (Try saying that out loud.)

Colton's face crumpled.

"I'm so sorry," Lexi said, immediately regretting her unkindness.

"Don't worry about it," said Colton. "It happens to me all the time."

What a sad experience! And even though Lexi felt terrible right after she said it, it was too late. Be kind to young men. Remember that they are often just as nervous as you are. If you need to turn a guy down, do it kindly.

Pitfall #2: Becoming Committed Too Soon

Lani—One of the hardest pitfalls for some to avoid is that of becoming committed too early. When you finally meet a guy who treats you with respect, you may want to grab on to him and hold on tight! But the right thing to do is to follow the counsel of modern prophets: Do not begin dating until sixteen, and do not pair off or steady date until you are at the appropriate age to be married.

Pitfall #3: Doing Something You Know Is Wrong in Order for a Guy to Like You

JOHN—One morning, while speaking to a radiant group of young women, I asked myself, Why would one of these wonderful young women choose to be immoral? They all seemed so confident, so full of goodness.

We think we found the answer to this question in a quote from President Ezra Taft Benson. He said, "Most people fall into sexual sin in a misguided attempt to fulfill basic human needs. We all have a need to feel loved and worthwhile. We all seek to have joy and happiness in our lives.

Timing Does Make a Difference!

Some people think that it doesn't matter when they start dating. Think again. One study (that included people who were members of the Church and those who were not) had the following results:

- Of the people who began dating at age twelve, 90 percent had had sex before graduating from high school.
- Of the people who began dating at age thirteen, 80 percent had had sex before graduating from high school.
- Of the people who began dating at age fourteen, 70 percent had had sex before graduating from high school.
- Of the people who began dating at age fifteen, 60 percent had had sex before graduating from high school.
- Of the people who began dating at age sixteen, 20 percent had had sex before graduating from high school.[1]

Notice the dramatic drop between fifteen and sixteen. Don't start dating earlier than you know is right just so some guy will like you. Do what is right; let the consequence follow!

Knowing this, Satan often lures people into immorality by playing on their basic needs. He promises pleasure, happiness, and fulfillment. But this is, of course, a deception."²

So President Benson taught that a major reason people are immoral is because they want to feel loved. I think this is also why a young woman might be tempted to date before she is sixteen or to steady date before graduating from high school. For some reason there is emptiness inside of her, and she wants to feel loved.

But no matter how you spin it, doing what is wrong does not bring love and acceptance. In fact, Elder M. Russell Ballard taught, "Transgression of any kind is always accompanied by a loss of self-esteem."³

President Benson gave the following outstanding counsel. We have memorized it, and we recommend that you do too!

"Do not be misled by Satan's lies. There is no lasting happiness in immorality. There is no joy to be found in breaking the law of chastity. Just the opposite is true. There may

Beware the pitfall of blaming guys for your misery. Or blaming guys if you are not getting asked out. Dress yourself up a little, develop talents, and be approachable and likeable so that you can be more attractive to guys. Remember the counsel from Sister Tanner's mother to "do everything you can to make your appearance pleasing, but the minute you walk out the door, forget yourself and start concentrating on others."⁴ There are some girls who don't do anything to improve their appearance. While guys do not care solely about physical attributes, physical attractiveness is still important to them. So make it important to you too, just not to excess.

Avoid the pitfalls!

be momentary pleasure. For a time it may seem like everything is wonderful. But quickly the relationship will sour. Guilt and shame set in. We become fearful that our sins will be discovered. We must sneak and hide, lie and cheat. Love begins to die. Bitterness, jealousy, anger, and even hate begin to grow. All of these are the natural results of sin and transgression."[5]

Don't fall into this trap! If a guy wants you to do something that you know is wrong, then he is not the guy for you! You can be the one to change the situation. As you stay true to what you know is right, you lay the foundation for a deeper and truer love. <u>True love is not giving up your virtue to please a boy.</u> President Kimball taught the following about true love: "Love is cleanliness and progress and sacrifice and selflessness. This kind of love never tires or wanes, but lives through sickness and sorrow, poverty and privation, accomplishment and disappointment, time and eternity."[6] If a boy is going to leave you because you won't be physical with him, you automatically know that *that* boy does not love you.

Know the difference!

Pitfall #4:
Being So Focused on Yourself
That You Forget Your Manners

Lani —While it's certainly important for young men to honor and respect you, you need to honor and respect them. And while this doesn't mean you have to open the door for them, there are simple courtesies you can extend that will help young men feel honored. Here are some examples.

Be ready on time. If a young man is going to pick you up at 7:00 P.M., be ready by 6:55 P.M. Don't force the poor guy to hang out with your great-uncle Rufus for twenty-five minutes while you finish getting ready for the night.

Unless it's absolutely necessary, *don't talk on the phone while you*

Avoid these Pitfalls!
- Being unkind to young men
- Becoming committed too soon
- Doing something you know is wrong in order for a guy to like you
- Being so focused on yourself you forget your manners

Be Ye Doers of the Word
- Set a goal not to steady date (or have a boyfriend) while you are in high school.
- Choose one of the other pitfalls we mentioned and make a plan for how you will avoid it.

THOUGHTS: _____
_____
_____
_____
_____
_____

are on a date. A book on teen manners put it this way: "If you make or take calls when you're in the middle of a face-to-face conversation, you're making whoever you're with feel second best."[7] The same rule applies to texting! One young man said, "If I'm on a date with a girl and she starts texting without even apologizing for being rude, I definitely won't be going out with her again."

Focus on the person you are with. If you're on a date with Guy #1, don't spend the evening flirting with Guy #2.

The main key is simply to follow the Golden Rule. *Treat others how you would like to be treated.* It isn't always easy to know what to do, but, honestly, most of the time it isn't that hard, either.

Notes

1. Carri P. Jenkins, "Making Moral Choices," *BYU Today*, April 1985, 39.
2. Ezra Taft Benson, "The Law of Chastity," *Brigham Young University 1987–88 Devotional and Fireside Speeches* (Provo: Brigham Young University, 1988), 50.
3. M. Russell Ballard, "Be an Example of the Believers," *Ensign*, November 1991, 97.
4. Susan W. Tanner, "The Sanctity of the Body," *Ensign*, November 2005, 15.
5. Benson, "The Law of Chastity," 51.
6. Spencer W. Kimball, *Faith Precedes the Miracle* (Salt Lake City: Deseret Book, 1972), 158.
7. Cindy Post Senning and Peggy Post, *Teen Manners: From Malls to Meals to Messaging and Beyond* (New York: HarperTeen, 2007), 46.

Chapter 9

What Should She Do?

In this chapter we'll tell you some stories that are based on true experiences. Then you'll be asked to finish the story by writing down how you think the character should respond and what happens as a result. Next, keep reading to find out what actually happened!

Case Study #1

Olivia has had a huge crush on Brandon for two years. Finally, during their senior year of high school, Brandon asked her out. Their first date was wonderful! Brandon met her family, played with her baby sister, and was a perfect gentleman all night. But on their second date, he began to do things that made her feel uncomfortable. He kept trying to hold her hand (even when she had her arms folded). At the end of the night, he asked if he could kiss her.

Olivia didn't want to kiss him yet (she had never kissed a guy), but she didn't know what to say. It was completely awkward, and even though she didn't say anything, Brandon started kissing her. Finally she pulled away and went in for the night.

Some of her friends say it's no big deal, and others say that she should avoid Brandon. It's easy to say, "Don't see Brandon," but Olivia is crazy about him. Plus, nobody else has asked her out for this Friday night, and Brandon is on the phone right now and wants to know if she will go to the movies with him.

You finish the story. What should Olivia do? What happens as a result of her choice?

_____

_____

_____

_____

_____

The Rest of the Story . . .

"So do you want to go this Friday?" Brandon said.

"No, thanks," Olivia replied.

"Why not?"

Olivia hesitated—should she lie or be truthful? "Honestly, Brandon, I didn't feel comfortable with how things went last time."

"What are you talking about?" Brandon said.

"Um . . ." This was embarrassing. "I guess I wasn't ready for you to kiss me and all that."

"Oh. I'm sorry. I didn't know you were like that," said Brandon.

"Like what?" Olivia asked.

"Like a Molly Mormon."

Olivia heard the phone click. He had hung up on her. She felt her cheeks getting hot, and tears came to her eyes. It was a very hard night, but she knew that she had done the right thing and had avoided a lot of future heartache by making the correct decision.

It was very difficult for Olivia to show respect for herself by holding true to what she felt good about. Have you had experiences in which it was tempting not to show respect for yourself? Satan tries to make people feel as though they are the bad ones when they do something right. Don't fall for this trap. It's great that Olivia expected the respect, and when it wasn't given to her, she didn't let the relationship continue.

Case Study #2

Emma's boyfriend, Austin, is the best and worst guy she has ever known. Sometimes he is like Prince Charming, always saying kind things to her and buying her presents. He always texts her little love messages, but when he is with her, sometimes he is just plain rude. More than once he has stood her up for a date, he often makes fun of her, and once he even slapped her. Twice Emma has broken up with him, but every time she does, she feels so lonely (no other guys are asking her out). Austin starts being sweet again, and they get back together. She wonders, *Maybe I should just be satisfied that I have a boyfriend, even if he isn't perfect. I mean, lots of other girls don't have anyone.*

You finish the story. What should Emma do? What happens as a result of her choice?

_____
_____
_____
_____

The Rest of the Story . . .

The Mutual theme a while back was "Be Strong and of a Good Courage." Emma was able to be strong—but not permanently. She broke up with Austin for four days, but she felt so lonely afterward. When he came back and asked if they could get back together, she gave in. Things went from bad to worse and, within a short period of time, she was pregnant, and Austin had left her. Her parents are supportive of her, but now she has some really difficult choices to make as far as what to do with her baby. She knows that her life will never be the same and that she made a really bad choice.

Remember what Elder Jeffrey R. Holland said, "In a dating and courtship relationship, I would not have you spend five minutes with someone who belittles you, who is constantly critical of you, who is cruel at your expense and may even call it humor."[1]

Please don't ever think that you deserve only guys who treat you like trash. Don't settle for someone who makes fun of you. You are divine—you deserve to be treated as such.

Case Study #3

Sarah feels as though her world is crashing down around her. She has had a tough life—her mother abandoned her at birth, and she spent the first five years of her life in foster homes. Then she was adopted by an LDS family, and for several years everything was wonderful. Now she is sixteen. It should be a sweet year, but it is turning bitter. Her adoptive parents are in the middle of a nasty divorce, and both are so wrapped up in their problems that neither wants custody of Sarah. She feels rejected—by both her birth and adoptive parents. *There must be something wrong with me*, she thinks. *Nobody wants to keep me.*

Sarah loves coming to Church but feels so disconnected from everybody else as she sits by herself. It seems as though all of the other young women are so much happier than she is and that they all have strong families. As she drifts on the edges of the Church, she always seems to get involved with guys who are jerks. *At least they pay attention to me,* she reasons. Sometimes she prays, but God just seems so distant. She wonders if it is worth the effort to keep on going.

You finish the story. If you were Sarah's friend, what would you tell her? What advice would you give her? What will happen if she follows your advice?

_____
_____
_____
_____
_____
_____
_____
_____
_____
_____

> We want you to take this to the next level! To see the rest of the story, head on over to http://johnhiltoniii.com/guys-girls. There you can submit the advice you would give to Sarah and view additional "What should she do?" scenarios. Go to the website and share your insights with us!

Note

1. Jeffrey R. Holland, "How Do I Love Thee?" BYU devotional address on 15 February 2000; http://speeches.byu.edu/reader/reader.php?id=1618&x=37&y=4; accessed 23 December 2010.

Conclusion

JOHN— In the introduction, I wrote about the opportunity I almost had to work in the Young Women program. If I were your Young Women leader, above all else, I think I would want to help you understand your deep worth as a daughter of God. I know that God loves you. Do you feel His love?

I spoke one time at a program called "Retreat for Girls." There were about one hundred young women there, and I invited them to write down questions they had, with the idea that I would answer them. I expected that only a few girls would ask questions, but more than fifty did. As I read through the questions, I was amazed at how deep many of them were. One question in particular deeply touched my heart. One young woman had asked, "How do I get my dad to love me?"

I cried as I read that question, and I attempted to answer it. I didn't know this girl, and I didn't know her dad. Hopefully he really does love her and is just having a hard time showing it. But oh, how my heart went out to that young woman. Although every daughter wants to feel the love of her earthly father, I hope that this young woman deeply feels the love that Heavenly Father has for her.

LANI— *We testify that Heavenly Father and Jesus Christ really do live. They know who you are and care about you personally. I want you to know* that I have no doubt that I really am a daughter of God! I am His daughter. I really am. I know you are His daughter! <u>He loves us and wants us to feel His love and to be respected.</u> ✳ Please *feel* that, please *know* that, and please *share* that truth with young women you interact with. Really, when a young woman knows who she is and expects to be treated as such, there is a power that will be in her life. She will be able to have greater confidence, be more concerned with others, and be truly happy. She will face school challenges with faith that her Father in Heaven will help her. She will be a stronger wife and a more loving mother! This knowledge is crucial to your happiness and obedience now and for the rest of your lives.

Please don't just know it or say it. Please internalize it, feel it, believe it, and act like it.

We'll conclude with three scriptures. Imagine that these are the words of the Lord spoken directly to you—because they are.

"I know thee by name" (Exodus 33:17).

"I have loved thee with an everlasting love" (Jeremiah 31:3).

"I will never leave thee, nor forsake thee" (Hebrews 13:5).

Date Night

Write down the following:

1. Name of a boy _____
2. Name of a girl _____
3. Adjective _____
4. Part of a house _____
5. Type of relative _____
6. Adjective _____
7. Name of a place _____
8. Adjective _____
9. Verb-ing _____
10. Verb-ing _____
11. Adjective _____
12. A period of time _____

Read this story, filling in the blanks with the words from above.

_____(1) drove up to _____(2)'s house. _____(2) was a very _____(3) young woman. _____(1) knocked on the _____(4). _____(2)'s _____(5) answered the door, and asked, "What do you want?" _____(1) felt really _____(6).

Just then _____(2) arrived. "Hi, _____(1)," she said. I'm so excited to go with you to _____(7). When they got to the car, _____(1) opened the car door for _____(2). "Thank you," she said. "You are very _____(8)."

As part of their date they had decided to spend some time _____(9). After that, they spent some time _____(10). At the end of the date, when _____(1) walked _____(2) to the door, both were feeling a little _____(11). After a good-night handshake, _____(2) walked inside. She hoped they would go on another date in _____(12).

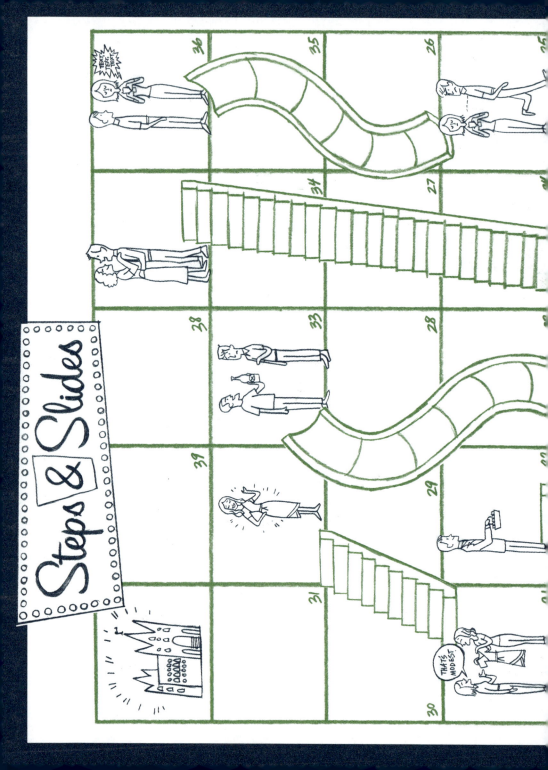

Fun Mutual Night Activity

We've got an idea that we think will help you have a *great* mutual night. Here's what you do:

Have a *brief* (five-minute) lesson on the importance of honoring and respecting womanhood.

Split everyone up into groups of six to eight people. Make movies based on the principles of girls expecting and accepting the respect and guys honoring women. (You can see examples of these videos at http://johnhiltoniii.com/guys-girls).

Upload your video to http://youtube.com. Send us a link and we'll post it at http://johnhiltoniii.com/guys-girls).

We can't wait to see your movie!

Why are you still holding this book? Go to http://johnhiltoniii.com/guys-girls and check it out!!!

What Guys Need to Know about Girls

are to God and attractive to you as they magnify their feminine traits and divinely given attributes of womanhood? You might even help mold the character and devotion of your own future eternal companion.[1]

That phrase "Will you begin a private crusade?" sounds to us like going to battle. We hope you will be like a stripling warrior—true at all times—and let each daughter of God feel what it is like to be in the presence of a priesthood holder who holds her in the proper esteem! Give her hope that guys who honor womanhood still exist! We promise that as you do your part to honor each young woman, you will feel of the love that Heavenly Father has for them, and for you. And that, dear brothers, is a marvelous feeling.

Note

1. Richard G. Scott, "The Sanctity of Womanhood," *Ensign*, May 2000, 36.

I didn't say anything, but I thought, *You could have said you're my friend!*

My point in sharing this story is this: It's one thing to talk about something, and it's quite another thing to do something. A lot of people talked to me the next day and said they were my friends. But only one person did something.

Lani — We've had a lot of fun writing this book, and we hope that you have enjoyed reading it. But more than that, we hope that you do things differently in your life because you've read it. Consider how these three scriptures relate to *doing*.

"If any man will do his will, he shall know of the doctrine, whether it be of God, or whether I speak of myself" (John 7:17).

"But be ye doers of the word, and not hearers only, deceiving your own selves" (James 1:22).

"Ye shall bind yourselves to act in all holiness before me" (D&C 43:9).

Throughout this book we have given you invitations to be "doers of the word." We invite you to think carefully about the things you have read. What will you do to show more honor and respect to your mother? To your sisters? To the other women you know?

I want to tell you that I know that Jesus Christ lives and is our Savior and Redeemer. He is the ultimate example of honoring women. I know this is something He cares about. If some of these principles seem too difficult right now, I know you will receive strength as you ask for God's help in implementing them.

John — Consider carefully this invitation from Elder Richard G. Scott:

> As a priesthood husband, father, son, or brother, each of us absolutely must help each daughter of God we can to realize what sacred characteristics Father in Heaven has given her. Will you begin a private crusade to help young women understand how precious they

Invitation to act!

Conclusion

JOHN — We'll conclude by sharing an experience that happened to me in junior high. Every day after school, my friends and I would hang out in one of the halls and just talk.

One afternoon I got into an argument with one of the guys in the group I'll call Steve. I don't remember what it was about. But the argument started to get pretty heated. Everybody else was watching us, and then Steve said, "John, why do you even hang out with us?"

"Because we're all friends."

"No, we're not!" Steve said. "None of us are your friends. Nobody here even likes you."

All of a sudden it was very quiet. "What do you mean?" I said. "We've been friends for forever." (I had known some of those people since I was three!)

Steve paused and looked around at everybody in the group. "Which one of you is friends with John? Tell me—is any of you John's friend?"

It was absolutely silent. After a long pause, one young man said, "I'm John's friend," and he and I walked off together.

The next day, several of the people who had been there the day before came up to me and said, "John, I'm so sorry about yesterday. Of course I'm your friend. I just didn't know what to say."

some of the people. For some reason, John thinks of a recent priesthood lesson on honoring women. *I should let her have my seat,* he thinks.

But at that exact moment, Hailey turns to John and says, "So, what are you doing this weekend?"

You finish the story. What should John do? What happens as a result of his choice?

_____

_____

_____

_____

_____

_____

_____

_____

_____

_____

_____

> We want you to take this to the next level! To see the rest of the story, head on over to http://johnhiltoniii.com/guys-girls. There you can submit what you think John should do and view additional "What should he do?" scenarios. Put down the book and share your insights with us!

What Guys Need to Know about Girls

The Rest of the Story

Lani — Now you can tell from the case study that there's a chance that Ryan is going to be unkind. But Ryan was a good guy. He realized that he was being selfish and that even though he didn't know Erika very well, he could still go out with her. After all, it was just one night, and she had made a big effort to invite him.

But it turned out that Ryan didn't have the opportunity to go to the dance with her. Erika's Homecoming was on a weekend when Ryan's family had already planned a trip that would take them out of town. Ryan told Erika this as gently as possible, but he could tell that she was disappointed. After that, though, he called Erika and invited her to do something with a group of his friends. Although it didn't work out for him to go to the dance, he worked hard to make sure that Erika still felt good about herself.

Case Study #3

John's heart is pounding. He has spotted Hailey, the girl he'd had a crush on since kindergarten, sitting at a table with some people from his ward. John doesn't usually sit with those guys, but today is the perfect day to start. There is only one seat left at the table, and it is the spot right next to her.

John carefully slides into the seat. Hailey smiles and nods at him, and John smiles back. John listens to the conversation and thinks about what he should do next. He feels a little uncomfortable at this table, but not because he doesn't like the people from his ward; it's just that he doesn't usually sit with them.

A couple of minutes later, John looks up and notices that another young woman from his ward, Sarah, is standing by the table, talking with

That gets Ryan's attention! When he gets to the bottom of the stairs, he sees two girls he doesn't know very well—Erika and Holly. They are girls that he had met at a church dance. They live in the stake next to his and go to a neighboring high school. Erika is holding a bouquet of balloons in her hand, and she gives them to Ryan.

It is an awkward situation. Ryan's parents and younger siblings are staring at him. Erika and Holly are staring at him. "Uh, thanks," Ryan says. He isn't sure what he is supposed to do.

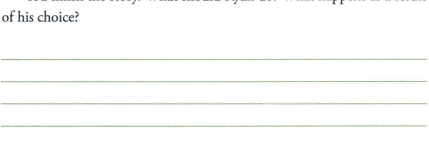

Holly helps him out: "You're supposed to pop the balloons to find a secret message."

Ryan begins popping the balloons. For some reason he feels very uncomfortable with everyone staring at him. *Great,* he thinks. *I don't even know these girls, and one of them is probably asking me to Homecoming or something. I wonder if I'm going to have to rent a tuxedo. That's a lot of money. And I wonder who will pay for dinner . . .*

The balloons get popped, and Ryan is right. Erika is asking him to her Homecoming. "Wow, thanks," Ryan says. But he isn't sure he means it.

You finish the story. What should Ryan do? What happens as a result of his choice?

What **Guys** Need to Know about *Girls*

The Rest of the Story . . .

Lani — Before we finish the story as it actually happened, you should know that Alex is a really incredible guy. He is diligent in church and considerate of others. But on this occasion, we think he made a bad move. He said, "Sorry, Jessica, I can't tonight. It's my night to hang out with the guys."

Young men, how do you think that made Jessica feel? She felt so hurt that she wrote, "I am never going to date another LDS guy." Now that is clearly not an appropriate response either, but our point is this: Alex's choice to hang out with the guys had an effect on Jessica that he might never be aware of. Are we aware of how our actions impact our female friends?

What could Alex have done instead? He could have graciously said yes and had a good time with Jessica. He also could have said, "Jessica, I'm so sorry that I'm not available tonight, but I would love to go out with you. Are you free tomorrow?" This would have allowed Alex to still hang out with the guys but also would have salvaged some of Jessica's esteem.

Case Study #2

Ryan is in eleventh grade. He is upstairs studying one night when he hears a knock at the front door. He ignores it, but soon hears his younger brothers and sisters calling, "Ryan, come down. There are some girls here!"

Chapter Nine

What Should He Do?

In this chapter, we'll present you with some case studies. The first two are based on true stories and the third, well, who knows, it might happen to you! After you read the case studies, you'll be asked to finish the story by writing down how you think the character should respond and what happens as a result. Next, keep reading to find out what actually happened!

Case Study #1

Alex has been home from his mission for a couple of months. He has not been on very many dates since his mission, but he is okay with that. In fact, he always looks forward to Friday nights because that's his night to hang out with the guys. Every Friday, he and a group of guy friends get together and watch a movie.

One Friday afternoon, Jessica, a girl from church, calls Alex and invites him to go to dinner with her. Alex does not know Jessica very well, and he really doesn't want to miss his movie night with the guys. On the other hand, he does not want to be rude, and he knows that "guys' night out" will continue with or without him.

You finish the story. What should Alex do? What happens as a result of his choice?

Bonus Scripture:

"Walk in the Spirit, and ye shall not fulfil the lust of the flesh."
—Galatians 5:16

BeWARE of:
1. Respecting only "beautiful" young women
2. Pushing respect
3. Pairing off too early
4. Sending the wrong message

Be Ye Doers of the Word

- Make a goal that you will not steady date until after your mission.
- Choose another pitfall from this chapter that you will take immediate action to avoid.

THOUGHTS:
_____
_____
_____
_____
_____
_____
_____
_____

Notes

1. Keith Morrison, "Face Value" (Dateline NBC, 13 January 2004); http://www.msnbc.msn.com/id/3917414/ns/dateline_nbc/; accessed 15 February 2011.
2. Gordon B. Hinckley, "Some Thoughts on Temples, Retention of Converts, and Missionary Service," *Ensign*, November 1997, 51.
3. Joshua Harris, *I Kissed Dating Goodbye* (Sisters, OR: Multnomah Publishers, 2003), 93.

level. When we went on our next date, it was clear to me that Catherine was willing to be a little more physical, but I felt that it would be more honorable and respectful not to kiss her, since we still didn't know each other very well.

As time went on, I found out that Catherine's parents were getting divorced, and that she really had an empty space in her life where she just wasn't feeling loved. I think that's why she was ready to be romantic physically, because she wasn't feeling enough emotional love from her parents. I never did kiss her, but I was always a good friend to her. I think I was able to show her real, genuine love (the friendship kind) because I didn't let things get physical.

Garrett set a great example by not sending the wrong signal, even though the girl seemed willing to share physical affection. Be honest in how you treat young women, and keep an eternal perspective.

These are some of the pitfalls to be avoided as you follow the path of honoring women. Avoid them—and you'll be glad you did!

Avoid the pitfalls!

What Guys Need to Know about Girls

One night, though, a bunch of my friends were going on a group date, and so I asked Katy. She was super friendly, and somehow during the date we started to hold hands. It felt really good, and I wanted to keep doing it.

So maybe I was being selfish—I don't know—but I decided just to hold hands with her all night. I figured, "Hey, it feels good to me, it feels good to her—why not?" At the time I didn't realize what it was meaning to her.

The next day, she came over to my house to talk. We went for a walk, and I could tell that she wanted to kiss me. I told her that I didn't think we should have that kind of physical relationship, and she got very upset. "Then why were we holding hands last night? Were you just using me?"

> Were you using me?

"No," I said. "I just thought we were both enjoying it. Can't we just hold hands and still be friends?"

"No!"

That night was a revelation to me. I realized that holding hands hadn't meant that much to me, but to her it meant commitment. Even though I wasn't trying to be hurtful, I was deceiving her by doing something physically that sent the wrong message to her. I decided that from that point on, I would be totally honest with girls by not sending them wrong signals.

This pitfall extends beyond physical affection to flirting or any other action that could lead a young lady on. A young man named Garrett shared this story:

I had been on a few dates with a young woman named Catherine. I liked being around her, and I was wondering if I should try to take things to the next

Within two years, Brian was married in the temple—and not to Brittany. "Brittany had stopped coming to church," Brian said. "Some terrible things happened to her and her family, and she felt lost. She really needed a friend in the Church to turn to, but she didn't have one. I wanted to help her, but things were too awkward between us."

"If Brittany and I had been 'just friends' in high school, I know I could have reached out to her," Brian said. "But because our relationship progressed too fast too soon, I wasn't able to be there for her when she really needed me."

Brian learned the hard way that a true warrior should put aside what he wants for what is best. Even if you feel unbelievably attracted to that special someone, show her that you really love her by avoiding the pitfall of pairing off.

Pitfall #4: Sending the Wrong Message

As we've already discussed, guys and girls are different. And they view physical things differently too. In his book *I Kissed Dating Goodbye,* Joshua Harris quotes a woman who says, "'Men tend to see the physical as more of an experience.' A girl's point of view is very different. . . . 'Kissing and "making out" mean something very precious and deep to a woman,' she said. 'It is our way of giving our trust, our love, our heart to the man we love. It leaves us very vulnerable.'"[3]

A young man we'll call Joseph shared a story that drives this point home.

> There was this girl, Katy, who really liked me. I was attracted to her physically, but we always argued about stuff, and I knew that we could never really be a couple—we were too different.

What *Guys* Need to Know about *Girls*

Besides the fact that the prophet said not to do it, there are lots of reasons to avoid steady dating:

- Steady dating limits your ability to meet new people.

- Steady dating limits *her* ability to meet new people. Would a warrior do that to a young woman?

- The chances of you doing anything immoral are much less if you do not steady date.

- Steady dating sets a bad example for the other young men in your quorums. Even if *you* weren't harmed by steady dating, your example could wreck the life of one of your priesthood brothers.

A young man we'll call Brian shared a story with us that gave us an additional perspective on why steady dating is a bad choice.

When Brian was a junior in high school, he fell in love with Brittany, a new girl in school. She returned his affection, and the two were as inseparable as peanut butter and jelly. They talked about marriage, they talked about how many children they would have—Brian truly could not imagine life without Brittany.

Brian decided to serve a mission, and Brittany promised to write him. Over the next two years, they wrote each other, but not as frequently as they thought they would. Brian became completely focused on missionary work, and Brittany was very involved in her university studies.

The night Brian got home from his mission, Brittany came to visit. It was very awkward. As they talked, Brian realized that they had grown in totally different directions. Shortly thereafter, Brian began school at a local college, and Brittany went back to her university.

Brian said, "Because we had always been boyfriend/girlfriend, it was really strange to talk with her, so I didn't. I just dropped her as a friend."

that's okay—*don't force them to take your respect. At the same time, don't get discouraged and stop trying to honor women.*

JOHN — It's also important to make sure you show respect in the right way. I was in the BYU bookstore one afternoon. I had recently given a talk telling young men to honor young women and to encourage young women to dress modestly.

A young man walked past me, talking on his cell phone. "Hey, Brother Hilton," he said. "Maybe you can help me. I'm trying to tell this girl to dress modestly but she won't listen to me. She's such a _____." (He then used a very offensive word that you should never use.)

Although I was happy this young man wanted his friend to dress modestly, he was going about it the wrong way. By aggressively telling her what to do (not to mention the name he called her), he may have been discouraging her from doing the right thing.

Pitfall #3: Pairing Off Too Early

There is a natural desire planted in man to have a deep and significant relationship with a woman. God made us that way so that we would desire marriage and family—it is part of His eternal plan.

Before your mission you may find yourself attracted to one particular young woman. You might have a lot in common and love being with her. She will probably love being with you. You will really like her. She will really like you. One of the biggest challenges you may have in honoring her is to make the decision not to pair off with her.

There's no doubt that the right thing to do is *not* to pair off. President Gordon B. Hinckley taught: "When you are young, do not get involved in steady dating. When you reach an age where you think of marriage, then is the time to become so involved. But you boys who are in high school don't need this, and neither do the girls."[2]

> **Be Like the Savior**
> "The Lord seeth not as man seeth; for man looketh on the outward appearance, but the Lord looketh on the heart."
> —1 Samuel 16:7

But we know that God does not look on the outward appearance (see 1 Samuel 16:7). So if we're going to be like Him, we shouldn't respect only some girls. We must honor all of them.

One young man said, "I know that I've fallen into the trap of respecting only girls I like or think are cute. I have had to make it a goal to go out of my way to respect any young woman—no matter what." That's a great suggestion for avoiding this pitfall.

Lani — A lot of girls I've talked to say that they are (very) impressed with *VERY!* young men who show respect to all women. They love it when a guy will be kind and gracious to everyone, not just the ones they like. They think that is the coolest thing ever.

Pitfall #2: Pushing Respect

Occasionally we'll talk to a young woman who says something like this: "I don't like it when guys open doors for me. Sometimes they'll even push me out of the way so that they can open it for me!" (We're not making this up!) While a young man who does this may feel he is doing the right thing, he has forgotten that the most important part of showing respect to a girl is to *put her needs first.* If a young woman wants to open her own door, respect that.

Another young woman told us an experience similar to the one above. She said that she did not mind having her door opened, but she just didn't want to be yelled at in order for it to happen.

Apparently some guys are a bit zealous in honoring young women! Although we personally believe young women should accept the respect offered by young men, you may meet a few who simply don't want it. And

Let's give you a situation, and you make a prediction. Two women are in New York City. One is a professional model, and the other is an employee of NBC (a secretary). They both have a folder full of papers, and they are going to drop them—sending the papers flying. The question is: Do you think more people will help the model or the secretary?

This test actually happened. As you might expect, people (especially men) flocked to help the model. A man even used his cane to keep some of the papers from blowing away.

But when the secretary dropped her folder, people kept walking by. After a dozen people ignored her, a woman finally helped.

That seems wrong, doesn't it? But for some reason, that kind of scenario happens more often than not. Here is an interesting side note: They did the same experiment with a male model and a male employee of NBC. Again many people helped the model, while the "regular" person was ignored![1]

Treating Each "Woman" Right

In John 2:4, the Savior called His mother "Woman." That might sound like a funny thing to call your mom, until you know that, in that period of time, the word "woman" was a title of respect. Here's what's even more interesting: In John 4:21, Jesus used this honorific title when referring to a lowly Samaritan woman, who was a complete stranger and of a nationality that most Jews despised and would normally not have anything to do with. And in John 8:10, when the Savior addressed the woman taken in adultery, He called her "Woman." Clearly, the Savior loved and respected every woman in the world, whether it was His own mother, a complete stranger, or a sinner. We should do likewise. We should respect all women—relatives, sinners, and strangers. (Yes, that means even girls you don't know or don't really care about.)

Chapter Eight

Potential Pitfalls

JOHN — You might think that when it comes to respecting young women, you can't go wrong. But we have found that there are a few potential pitfalls that you might want to avoid. Here are some things to beware:

- Respecting only "beautiful" young women.
- Pushing respect.
- Pairing off too early.
- Sending the wrong message.

Let's check them out.

Pitfall #1: Respecting Only "Beautiful" Young Women

Lani — One young woman said, "I think guys are nice only to the pretty girls. I've seen guys go out of their way to be nice to a cute girl, but totally ignore her friend who might not be quite as attractive. That's not right!"

JOHN — What do you think of that accusation? Does it ring true?

- Girls really aren't a mystery. If you still aren't sure what they want, go back and read this chapter again!

Be Ye Doers of the Word
- Choose one piece of advice given by a young lady in this chapter and act on it!
- Commit to never talk dirty or rudely—especially around girls.

THOUGHTS:
_____
_____
_____
_____
_____
_____
_____
_____

Bonus Scripture:

"Neither filthiness, nor foolish talking, nor jesting, which are not convenient."
—Ephesians 5:4

Notes

1. Jeff Feldhahn and Eric Rice, with Shaunti Feldhahn, *For Young Men Only: A Guy's Guide to the Alien Gender* (New York: Multnomah Books, 2008), 18, 30.
2. Dallin H. Oaks, "Dating versus Hanging Out," *Ensign*, June 2006, 13.

twenty-four hours and then comments and likes every single thing you post on Facebook, and if he is always around you and you just met him once . . . that is awkward and not comfortable. It puts us in a difficult situation because we want to take things slow! So please, boys, don't stalk girls!"—Grace

Be Kind—Especially When You Are with Your Guy Friends

"When you are with your guy friends, don't ignore the girls. Don't forget to be gentlemen. Still open doors whether you are with your friends or not."—Claire

"It seems like standing when a girl enters a room is appropriate when you are greeting someone. I like it when the guys get off the couch and give me a hug to greet me. Now, it would be absolutely amazing if they paused their video game when I came in."—Lily

"It is not fun when you are on a date with a guy, and they are always off with other people, and you have to go find them all of the time, especially at dances."—Emma

"I think chivalry is good. I think that some guys don't show respect to girls because they are scared. They seem particularly scared of what their friends might think of them or call them."—Alyssa

JOHN— So there you have it, warriors—words of wisdom straight from young ladies to you. Now we should warn you: relationships with ladies aren't just fun and games. There are some potential pitfalls that you need to avoid—and that's the subject of our next chapter.

"I really do not like it when guys try to show respect in a commanding way by yelling, 'Don't move! I am going to get your chair for you.' I don't feel respected; I feel like I am not being given a choice. It is much better if they say, 'I'd love to get that for you,' or 'Oh, let me get that for you,' in a kind, gentle way."—Elizabeth

"Be socially competent. By that I mean, if you are talking to children, then know how to play with children. If you are in a serious, reverent place, know how to be serious. Know that there is a time and a place to be fun and a time and a place to be serious. Looks don't matter if you have those things."—Madison

Really Listen

"Boys should just listen rather than try to solve problems. Sometimes girls just want to talk, and it is really nice when boys will just listen."—Katelyn

Check out his EARS!

WHY DO SO MANY GIRLS LIKE THAT GUY?

"It is fine to text, but when you are with a girl, especially on a date, you should be paying attention to the girl, not texting. You need to be able to be in a conversation and really listen, not just nod your head and be thinking about other things, but to really listen."—Sierra

"I like it when guys will stop what they are doing to listen and give their full attention to you."—Amber

Don't Be a Creeper

"Don't be creepy stalkers. Girls are friendly, and we want to have good friends, but if a boy starts calling or texting you day and night, when you accept him on Facebook and he comments on all your pictures in the first

What Guys Need to Know about Girls

"Come sit by us once in a while. It's fun to sit by guys, but I don't feel like I can always initiate it."—Summer

You Are Awesome

"Boys should be more confident. Ninety percent of the time girls will be nice, so please ask us out!"—Brianna

"Guys should know that we girls like it when they are themselves. We don't like it very much when they try to be someone they're not, and we can tell when they aren't being themselves!"—Kylie

"Boys should know how great they are, and how awesome we think they are for holding the priesthood. How thankful we are to them for offering the sacrament, which is an ordinance we all need."—Emily

> Guys, girls really want us to emphasize this point: Ask girls on dates! Elder Dallin H. Oaks said that "men have the initiative," so step up to the plate![2]

STEP UP TO THE PLATE

Don't Be Afraid to Be Polite

"I love boys who are really polite, who open doors all the time for me—not just on dates. I love it when they help those who are lonely or don't have friends."—Sophie

"Do what your mother taught you. Mind your manners! If your mother did not teach you, then learn some manners. Open doors for girls. Know to put the napkin in your lap. Do the old-fashioned things. A few good manners can go a long way to impress a girl."—Kristen

"Girls like guys who are mature, respectful, and socially competent. They like guys who don't talk about stupid things. Don't treat girls like you would your buddy. Don't call them 'dude.'"—Brooke

"Be chivalrous! What does that mean? Try to make girls happy and comfortable. Look out for her needs. If the girl is happy, the guy is usually happy."—Amy

Be Modest

"No low pants! It's not attractive at all. No shaggy hair—it looks sloppy. Be modest in what you do and say. Wear your shirt and use good language."—Rachael

"Guys should be modest in language and actions. They shouldn't be hypocritical and tell us to be modest when they are not. It is kind of awkward when they don't have a shirt on."—Megan

"Some guys think it is all cool to take off their shirts. I am so not impressed by that."—Gabriela

Don't Do Weird Stuff

"This is crazy to say, but I'm around a lot of guys who burp and make other gross noises. What is up with that? Don't do that!"—Abbie

"I know a lot of guys like video games, but when I hear guys talking about games or movies where they were killing people or blood was everywhere, that is just gross. I don't want to hear about it."—Carly

"You can't treat girls the way you treat your guy friends. Don't wrestle with them or do all the weird things guys do."—Belle

Talk to Us

"Sometimes guys just hang out with other guys, and it seems like they are afraid of us girls. Don't be afraid—we want to talk to you!"—Ann

"Girls really do love it when guys are spiritual and answer questions in church. To me, it's very impressive, and it shows they aren't scared of what people will think. It's great when a guy shows confidence and is willing to just come say 'Hi.'"—Kayla

"Guys could do a little better about telling the girl about the date. Don't call her a half an hour before you pick her up and say it is going to be a casual (or formal) activity."—Jessica

"Dating is about getting to know lots of other people. It is not all about going out with the best-looking girl. Take the opportunity to ask out girls who could benefit from associating with a good guy. It is not always about romance. It is about what you learn."—Heather

"On dates, if you let the girl see an example of how they should be treated, that is how they will expect to be treated in the future."—Nicole

Little Things Mean More Than You Think

"Guys should know girls need tenderness. They like simple things like notes and flowers, helping her with her coat, and opening the door. That is what girls go crazy about and will go home and talk about."—Michelle

"Notice little things. Once a guy noticed I had new earrings. I thought that was so neat he would notice, and then he listened to my long story of how I got them. That was so nice."—Brittney

"Little things can mean a lot more than really big expensive things. Simple things like a wildflower, a note on a locker, or a note in a random place asking how things are going can mean a lot more than tickets to an expensive show."—Olivia

Chivalry Is Always In

"Chivalry is never overrated. You should open the door and be polite. Don't be afraid to show you are spiritual. We like to see it, and sometimes we cannot tell unless you really show it and express it. Be an example of the believers."—Kelsey

"Girls like gentlemen. It is nice for the guy to be humble and meek, not condescending and conceited."—Jamie

want to know the truth even if we ask for it. I know it sounds crazy, but it is true."—Savannah

"If you notice a girl is sad, say something. Go up to her and ask her if something is wrong and can you do something to help. That is what means the most to me—when guys really care about my feelings. I love that."—Lauren

Be Kind with Your Words

"I don't think guys realize how much what they say affects girls' self-esteem. Guys would joke about me being overweight in eighth grade, and then they said I was too skinny in ninth grade. They couldn't make up their minds! So I had an eating disorder."—Maria

> *Girls, pay attention!! No matter what a guy says, there is never a good reason for an eating disorder. If you struggle with an eating disorder, please talk with your parents.*

"If I were dressed in a way that was inappropriate, I would want a guy to tell me in a kind way. I would want to know. Not all girls are like that though. You really have to be sensitive"—Ali

Be kind!

"A nice, sincere compliment goes a long way."—Katie

"Tell us we are beautiful."—Jocie

"I don't think girls can ever get enough compliments."—Amelia

Dating Do's and Don'ts

"High school is a time to have fun, not for pairing off. Girls like to be in different situations. We don't want to go to a movie all the time."—Angela

"It is not how extravagant the date was, it is the little things that stand out the most. Let a girl see your true self."—Liz

"You don't always have to pay, but it is nice when you offer."—Hailey

talked with lots of young women and asked them what they wish you guys knew. These responses are straight from the mouths of young women.

Treat Us Like Princesses

"Treat us like princesses: open doors, show respect."—Wendy

"Be aware, attentive, and respectful. If she's carrying a heavy bag, offer to help her with it. If she is cold, offer her your coat. Notice stuff. If she needs something, offer to help. If it is icy and slippery, offer your arm. That is always nice."—Sarah

Galatians 6:2!

"Courtesy is number one. Be considerate of our needs. Put our needs first."—Hannah

"Thoughtfulness. I don't think any man can be too considerate of a woman. It doesn't mean you have to go out and buy expensive gifts. Bring her a flower from your yard. It is not always in words; it is in doing."—Lacy

Respect Our Wishes—Physically

"I think guys should care about our salvation. Even if they know we are going to be someone else's wife, they can still care about our salvation."—Lindsay

"Respect our limits. If the girl doesn't want to kiss, be okay with that. Or if she says no to something else, respect that."—Ashley

"If you are going to give a hug, give a quick hug—no back rubs and no lingering."—Ellie

Be Sensitive to Our Feelings

"You need to be aware of how girls think. You may say something and not realize that it hurt the girl. When we say, 'Do you like my new haircut?' don't say, 'Well, I really liked the old one better.' Often we don't

Chapter Seven

What Girls Wish Guys Knew

JOHN—Some guys might be reading this book and thinking to themselves, *I wish I were better looking—then more girls would like me!*

But consider this:

In one survey, girls were asked, "Suppose you had a choice to go out with one of two guys at school who you don't know very well—Guy A or Guy B. Guy A is so good-looking that he could be a magazine model, and he is captain of the football team, but you have heard through the grapevine that 'he thinks he's all that.' Guy B is only average-looking, but you have heard through the grapevine that he's a nice guy who has a funny sense of humor. Both seem to have quite a few friends, and both are interested in going out with you, but you have to choose only one and not the other. Which one do you choose?"

In answering this question, 91 percent of girls said they would choose Guy B. Most guys will be amazed by that fact, but the truth is, girls care a lot more about a guy's personality than his looks. In fact, in one study more than 90 percent of girls said that if a guy wanted to make a good impression on girls, it would be more important for him to improve his inner qualities than to work out in the gym.[1]

That should be good news to most young men! What's on the outside doesn't matter as much as what's on the inside! For this chapter, we've

not to take. To love is to serve, not to exploit. . . . The young man who protects his sweetheart against all use or abuse, against insult and infamy from himself or others, could be expressing true love. But the young man who uses his companion as a biological toy to give himself temporary satisfaction—that is lust.[5]

Be a true man and protect the virtue of women.

We hope this chapter hasn't been too heavy for you—but we wanted to say it straight. Although the world tells you that to be a man you should be immoral, a real man stays sexually pure. We promise you that you will be eternally grateful for your choice to live the law of chastity.

Notes

1. *For the Strength of Youth* (Salt Lake City: The Church of Jesus Christ of Latter-day Saints, 2001), 27.
2. Glenn L. Pace, "Spiritual Revival," *Ensign*, November 1992, 11–12.
3. Edward L. Kimball, ed., *The Teachings of Spencer W. Kimball* (Salt Lake City: Bookcraft, 1982), 281.
4. Dan Ariely, *Predictably Irrational: The Hidden Forces That Shape Our Decisions* (New York: HarperCollins, 2008), 101.
5. Spencer W. Kimball, *Spencer W. Kimball* [manual], in Teachings of Presidents of the Church series (Salt Lake City: The Church of Jesus Christ of Latter-day Saints, 2006), 182.

- You can stay sexually pure by creating a "hedge" to keep yourself from getting too close to the "ledge."

Be Ye Doers of the Word

- Pray and talk to Heavenly Father about what hedges you should create for yourself to keep from ever getting close to the ledge.
- Share what you've learned from this chapter with a friend who needs it.

THOUGHTS:
_____
_____
_____
_____
_____
_____
_____
_____

In other words, things that they would have never done while in a calm rational state, they would do when they were aroused.

He summarized his research by saying, "Teenagers . . . <u>must walk away from the fire of passion</u> before they are close enough to be drawn in. Accepting this advice might not be easy, but our results suggest that it is easier for them to fight temptation before it arises than after it has started to lure them in. In other words, avoiding temptation altogether is easier than overcoming it."[4] Keep in mind that this is a non-LDS scientist at one of America's most prestigious universities telling teenagers that they need to create boundaries to keep from going too far. This is why we need that hedge—to avoid getting into a state where we make foolish decisions.

Walk away!

> ### Beware of the Aggressive Girl!
>
> One danger you will face is the aggressive girl. She might actively tempt you and tell you (with words or actions) that she wants to do things that you know are wrong. This situation isn't new—remember that Potiphar's wife aggressively tried to put the moves on Joseph, but he "fled, and got him out" (Genesis 39:12). When a girl aggressively pursues you physically, be a true man and get out of that situation.

JOHN— Guys, let's be blunt. If you really love a girl, you will protect her virtue. Mormon wrote that chastity is "most dear and precious above all things" (Moroni 9:9). President Spencer W. Kimball said this of boys who would try to rob a girl of her virtue:

> Their lips say, "I love you." Their bodies say, "I want you." Love is kind and wholesome. To love is to give,

What Guys Need to Know about Girls

window and thought, "That looks kind of fun out there. This train is so restrictive." So we have jumped off and gone and played in the woods for a while. Sooner or later we find it isn't as much fun as Lucifer makes it appear or we get critically injured, so we work our way back to the tracks and see the train ahead. With a determined sprint, we catch up to it, breathlessly wipe the perspiration from our forehead, and thank the Lord for repentance....

I would propose that the luxury of getting on and off the train as we please is fading. The speed of the train is increasing. The woods are getting much too dangerous, and the fog and darkness are moving in.[2]

Does that make sense? The world is becoming increasingly wicked. It is harder to repent than it once was. Flirting with the ledge really can hurt you. Make a hedge!

Some interesting research has recently been done that helps us understand why a hedge is so important. A social scientist at the Massachusetts Institute of Technology asked college students questions about sexual issues under two sets of circumstances. First, he had them answer these questions when they were in a calm, rational state. Then, at a later time, he had them answer the questions while they were in a state of arousal. He found that their answers were very different when they were in a state of arousal.

High School Kissing

President Kimball said, "To kiss in casual dating is asking for trouble."[3] Since most, if not all, dating in high school should be casual, what implications does that have?

Hmm... NO!!!

land on those spikes. Obviously, it's incredibly foolish to spend time close to the ledge.

The hedge represents barriers that you put in place to keep yourself from getting too close to the ledge. As long as you stay on the correct side of the hedge, you don't have to worry about falling off the ledge.

When it comes to the law of chastity, the prophet has given us very clear guidance as to where the ledge is. *For the Strength of Youth* says, "Before marriage, do not do anything to arouse the powerful emotions that must be expressed only in marriage. Do not participate in passionate kissing, lie on top of another person, or touch the private, sacred parts of another person's body, with or without clothing. Do not allow anyone to do that with you."[1] If we cross this line, we are falling toward the spikes below.

Lani — *Guys, you need to create a "hedge" for yourself to keep from ever getting close to the "ledge." A "hedge" is a personal standard that you set that will keep you from getting close to the line of sin. You can pray and get personal revelation on what these hedges should be for you. For example, maybe one of your hedges could be, "I'll never be alone in the car (or a house) with a member of the opposite sex." Another hedge could be, "I will tell my mom about everything I do physically with a girl." We're not saying you need to set these specific hedges, we are just encouraging you to pray and talk with God about the specific hedges you should set for yourself.*

Sometimes guys (and girls) think, *Well, I can just have a little fun now and repent later. I can slide down the cliff just a little bit and not get hurt too badly by the spikes. I'll just climb out later.* Elder Glenn L. Pace used an analogy of a train to help us realize that this is not true. He said:

> It is as if we are passengers on the train of the Church, which has been moving forward gradually and methodically. Sometimes we have looked out the

Chapter Six

What about Kissing?

JOHN— Okay, guys, it's time for a man-to-man talk.

Lani— May I join in too?

JOHN— Okay, we'll have a man-to-man-with-a-woman-also-in-the-conversation talk. When it comes to sexual purity, there is a simple concept that we want to teach you. Our friend Brent Fillmore taught it to thousands of youth and we hope that it will be helpful to you. Take a look at this drawing:

We don't expect you to read everything we wrote to the girls, but we do recommend you at least read the chapter "What about Kissing?" on the flip side of this book. It has some important information we didn't include in this chapter.

Notice that there is a hedge, a ledge, and spikes at the bottom that will hurt or kill anyone who lands on them. This picture is like the law of chastity. Simply put, if you break the law of chastity, it is like landing on spikes. *It will hurt you.*

The ledge represents the line of sin. Some people play around by the ledge, hoping they won't go "too far." Maybe they think, *I can always repent later.* They don't understand the pain that comes when you

- You can honor women in so many ways! Give a compliment, offer them your seat, open the door for them—you can do it!

Be Ye Doers of the Word

- Choose one way you can honor the women you associate with. Now go do it!
- Give a compliment to each woman you see today, regardless of her age. Be sincere.

THOUGHTS:

_____
_____
_____
_____
_____
_____
_____
_____
_____
_____

Bonus Scripture:

"And whatsoever you do, do it heartily, as to the Lord."
—Colossians 3:23

Notes

1. M. Russell Ballard, "Here Am I, Send Me," BYU devotional address, 13 March 2001; http://speeches.byu.edu/reader/reader.php?id=926&x=46&y=3; accessed 22 December 2010.
2. Gordon B. Hinckley, "Your Greatest Challenge, Mother," *Ensign*, November 2000, 97.
3. David L. Beck, "The Magnificent Aaronic Priesthood," *Ensign*, May 2010, 56.
4. Gregory A. Prince and William Robert Wright, *David O. McKay and the Rise of Modern Mormonism* (Salt Lake City: University of Utah Press, 2005), 384.
5. M. Russell Ballard, "Purity Precedes Power," *Ensign*, November 1990, 37.
6. Richard G. Scott, "The Sanctity of Womanhood," *Ensign*, May 2000, 37.
7. Ibid.
8. David O. McKay, *David O. McKay* [manual], in Teachings of the Presidents of the Church series (Salt Lake City: The Church of Jesus Christ of Latter-day Saints, 2003), xv.
9. *For the Strength of Youth*, (Salt Lake City: The Church of Jesus Christ of Latter-day Saints, 2001), 22.
10. http://www.scribd.com/doc/27304902/United-States-Marine-Mcrp-6-11b-20-October-1998; accessed 12 January 2011.

What *Guys* Need to Know about *Girls*

We mention this story not because you necessarily need to peel mangoes, but to show that there are some unique deeds that certain cultures, or individual girls, will appreciate. You might not even like mangoes or live in a place where people eat mangoes, but you should look for small and simple things you can do that will help communicate to women that they truly do have a divine nature and destiny.

Feel It in Your Heart

Lani — With all of these courtesies, the most important factor is that the intent of your heart is right. You can open a door out of obligation, or you can open it because you feel respect and honor in your heart. Believe it or not, most times girls will be able to tell the difference. I have had the experience of someone opening the door for me, and I felt like it was done with little thought. On other occasions, I have felt honor and respect from the same simple gesture.

Where's the beef?

John — We've talked about a lot of small things in this chapter. Will doing these simple courtesies really make a difference? They will! Remember, "by small and simple things are great things brought to pass" (Alma 37:6). We invite you to take a couple of minutes to ponder which of the simple courtesies you can start doing right now. We promise that as you do more of these small and simple things you will feel more of the Spirit of the Lord in your life. It will bless your own life and it will bless the lives of the women around you.

It is not just what is on the outside that counts!

to their moms, the responses are awesome, especially the ones the young men come up with:

- Text her "I love you"
- Do chores without being asked
- Make her dinner
- Remember her birthday and Mother's Day
- Give her a hug
- Tell her she is beautiful
- Write her a note of appreciation
- Don't argue with her
- Ask for her advice or opinion and follow it

The ultimate example of a person honoring his mother is our Savior Jesus Christ. Not only was He willing and eager to help His mother in everyday life (read John 2:3–11 to see the first of all the miracles He performed), but He even looked out for her during His most difficult and challenging time (see John 19:26–27). Maybe it is easy for you to show respect to your mom when all is going well. But what about when nothing is going your way, you're frustrated with school, work, and friends, and even your mom seems to be getting on your nerves? I invite you to follow the Savior's example of looking out for your mom even on the hardest days.

"Peel the Mango"

JOHN — Wu Cuiling, a young woman living in China, told me that she felt respected by a young man when he would peel her mango for her. I thought that was very interesting! I don't eat mangoes very often, but I have always asked Lani to peel my oranges because she is much faster at it than I am. Lani assures me that she's not offended, but this idea of "peeling the mango" got me thinking. It is such a small thing, yet to Wu Cuiling it was important.

What *Guys* Need to Know about *Girls*

Lani—I love this experience because sometimes people think that common courtesy is reserved only for Mormon circles or certain cultures, but there we were in Mexico being taught something that was common knowledge and an absolute must to Javier. It still brings a smile to my face that men around the world do know and act appropriately toward women (even when Hollywood sure makes it seems otherwise).

Offer Your Seat

John—I was reading about unwritten rules for Marines and found this statement: "On a bus or street car, a Marine always gets up and offers his seat to a woman with packages or children, an elderly lady, or a pregnant woman."[10] That is great advice for every young man! When there are not enough chairs set up for Sunday School or a Mutual activity, or even in a high school class, you should take the initiative to set up more chairs for the ladies or give up your own, whichever will show more kindness to her.

> Good manners are not reserved for dates only! These courtesies are even more effective in daily life, and that is the best way to get in the habit of doing them. They are to be used at home, school, and church activities, and not just on rare occasions. They are not just for Marines either!

Treat Your Mother with Respect

Lani—Girls notice how you treat your mother and other women in your family! But even without that bit of incentive, you should give your mom respect. Not only do you owe her a lot, but she is usually around to practice on. When I ask youth to share ideas of how they can show respect

Don't Put Us Down—Even in Joking

Lani — I know that guys love to be funny. And I appreciate humor. But, men, you have to know that young women talk differently than young men do. Young men sometimes say things like, "You're so dumb. Just joking. Ha ha." Maybe you are joking, and maybe your guy friends understand that. But it can be really hurtful to girls. Remember, *For the Strength of Youth* says, "Do not insult others or put them down, even in joking. Speak kindly and positively about others."9

John — I can still recall when Elder Kenneth Johnson of the Seventy came and visited my mission. He made a simple statement that I've always remembered. He said, "You don't talk to sisters like you talk to elders." That is a basic but true point. You don't talk to girls the same way you talk to guys. Whether you are with girls or just with your guy friends, don't ever put young women down, even if you are joking. You can still get their attention —just be positive.

Walk on the Curb Side of the Street

I didn't learn about this simple idea until just after I was married. Lani and I were living in Mexico, and we would frequently walk together to our work at a university. Javier, who worked with us, joined us one day. We were walking like this.

Javier rebuked me by saying, "John, if you are not going to treat your wife with respect, then I will!" He then moved so that he was the person closest to the street.

I didn't know what I was doing wrong, but he explained to me that when walking on the street with a woman, the man should walk on the side closest to the street, thus protecting her from any traffic.

Don't Forget about Your Sister!

As you think about simple courtesies, remember that you can and should practice them on your sisters. Elder Richard G. Scott said, "As a brother, you can have a powerful, positive influence in your sister's life. . . . Simple courtesies like opening the door for her and building her self-esteem will encourage her to find her real worth."[7]

President David O. McKay told youth, "I remember my father's admonition when I started in my teens to court a young girl: 'David, you treat that young lady as you would have any young boy treat your sister.'"[8]

The Apostle Paul said we should treat "the elder women as mothers; the younger as sisters, *with all purity*" (1 Timothy 5:2; emphasis added). We should treat young women like we would our sisters, by guarding their purity and keeping them safe.

> How do you want a guy to treat your sister?

Sometimes I will go up to one of those young men. Our conversation might go like this:

Me: "Would you like to ask a young lady to dance?"

Young man: "No."

Me: "Why not?"

Young man: "Because I don't feel like dancing."

I feel like saying, "Who cares if you don't feel like it? Open your eyes and look at all of the young women who are basing their self-esteem on whether or not a young man asks them to dance."

Once I sat with two young ladies who weren't getting asked to dance. "What do we have to do to get a guy to ask us to dance?" one asked.

"Well, you could make a sign or something," I joked.

On the next slow song, I watched the girls. They didn't have a sign, but they stood on the dance floor, and each girl was pointing at herself and mouthing the words, "Pick me!"

Fortunately, they were asked to dance. But no girl should have to advertise herself just to be asked to dance. Young men, if you go to a dance, dance. Set a goal for yourself that you will ask girls to dance. You don't have to marry them, or even like them. Do it because you're a warrior who wants each young lady at the dance to have a good time.

Offer to Help Her with Her Coat or Carry Her Things

Lani—I remember the first time someone helped me with my coat. I really did not know what to do. The young man held the collar of my coat up behind me so I could slip one arm in each sleeve. I thought it was the kindest gesture ever, and I felt like a queen! I feel similarly honored when a guy asks if he can assist me in any way. It is classy. In general, girls are capable of getting their own coats, carrying their own things, opening their own doors, but it is certainly a kind gesture when the guy offers!

young lady feel of her self-worth as a daughter of God, not for you to get attention.

Open the Door

Opening the door is a simple, but much appreciated courtesy to a woman. As you approach a door, just make sure you are a step ahead so that you can easily open it for her. If you arrive at the door at the same time, it can be awkward, but if you're a step ahead she will likely sense that you are going to open it for her. Sometimes opening car doors can be a little tricky.

Yes, it is! It is <u>easy</u> to open the car door for a woman when you are getting in. Just walk to her door first and reach your hand out ahead of hers. Opening her door on the way out of the car can be a little tougher—but do it! As you stop the car, look at her and say, "If you don't mind waiting a second, I'd love to get your door." That way, she is not left guessing as to what you will do. This will help you both feel more comfortable.

Just Talk to Us and Listen to What We Have to Say!

Lani—Guys, I'll let you in on a little secret. Most girls love to talk! Sometimes one of the nicest courtesies you can extend is to have a genuine conversation with a young woman. Really listen to her. You don't have to solve all her problems—just listening makes a big difference.

And, yes, this means no texting while you are talking or listening. One girl shared how hurt she felt when she was expressing her feelings, and the guy looked at her and nodded, but was obviously trying to carry on two conversations at the same time as he texted away. She did not like it one bit!

Ask Us to Dance

JOHN—One of the saddest things to see at a youth dance is young women sitting on the sidelines and young men getting drinks or eating food.

Give Compliments

It's important to compliment women and girls, especially your sisters. As Elder Richard G. Scott said, "As a brother, you can have a powerful, positive influence in your sister's life. Compliment her when she looks especially nice. She may listen to you more than to your parents when you suggest that she wear modest clothing."⁶

Lani—Compliment her hair, her eyes, her modest dress, the way she builds others, the way she lives her testimony, her actions, her personality, the way she uses her time, her humility, her leadership, her unselfishness, her service, and her smile. The sky is the limit. We are not thinking of pick-up lines here. This is not something to be held back. Find any kind word and say it.

John—Do you remember the story we told about our three-year-old daughter in the introduction? I was surprised that the lack of compliments would affect even a little girl. And if it would affect a little girl, then it certainly affects teenage girls and even older women! One of the simplest and most effective ways you can show respect to the women in your life is to compliment them.

Pull Out Her Chair

Be careful with this one! This isn't the "pull out the chair so they fall down" trick that you might have played in elementary school. This simply means that when you are sitting down together, you pull out her chair and gently push it in as she sits down.

Not all young women will be used to a young man helping her with her chair. So you might want to say, "Let me get your chair for you," so she knows you are helping her, and not just getting a seat for yourself. If she doesn't realize what you are doing and pulls out her own chair instead, don't mention it—remember, the goal is to help this

had been taught the doctrine before, but it wasn't until she was treated differently that she really felt it. As a young man, you can help young women feel that they are daughters of God by how you treat them. President Gordon B. Hinckley said that young men need to be taught "to respect young women as daughters of God endowed with something very precious and beautiful."[2]

Young Men general president David L. Beck said, "A faithful priesthood man . . . will treat every young woman with kindness and respect."[3] You can be a faithful priesthood man!

Elder Robert L. Simpson related the account of how President David O. McKay honored his wife. Elder Simpson said, "I remember that we [he and President McKay] were out at a cemetery, and it was a blustery, wintry day. His white hair was blowing in the wind. As he approached the car, one of his attendants . . . [took] Sister McKay around the other side of the car to help her in. He said, 'Just a minute, hold on there.' And he walked all the way around the car with this cold wind blowing, and he opened the door for Emma Ray, and he said, 'This is my responsibility,' and he helped her in. Here he was, ninety years old. It was a great lesson."[4]

Elder M. Russell Ballard explained, "You young men must cultivate a considerate attitude toward women of all ages. The young women asked me to tell you that they want you to respect them and show them common, sincere courtesy. <u>Do not hesitate</u> to show your good manners by opening a door for them, taking the initiative to invite them on a date, and standing as they enter a room. Believe it or not, in this age of equal rights, the young women want you to extend these simple courtesies."[5]

No hesitating!

What are the "simple courtesies" we should extend to young women? We have asked hundreds of young women what young men could do to show them respect. Here are some of their answers.

Chapter Five

How to Treat a Young Woman Like a Pearl of Great Price

JOHN—Once we've decided to be righteous warriors who will honor and respect young women, we need to know how to do it. How can we treat young women like the pearls of great price that they really are?

Elder M. Russell Ballard answered this question simply by saying, "Let the women in your life know that you want them to be women of God and not women of the world."[1]

We shared this quote with some young women and asked, "How would you feel if a guy came up to you and said, 'I want you to be a woman of God and not a woman of the world'?"

They laughed, because that's not something that you hear a guy say every day. One young woman suggested, "It might be better if guys did things to let us know we were respected as women of God, rather than just tell us what they want us to be or do."

We think that this is what Elder Ballard meant—what you say is important, but what you do is even more important. This point was driven home to us during a testimony meeting at a youth conference when we heard a young woman say, "My testimony of who I am as a daughter of God has increased this week because of how the young men treated me."

We realized that the actions of those young men had, in fact, helped this young woman want to be a woman of God. It is interesting that she

Bonus Scripture:

"Speaking the truth in love."
—Ephesians 4:15

- Pornography is evil. Avoid it at all costs.
- Help young women by encouraging them (with your words <u>and</u> your actions) to dress modestly.

Be Ye Doers of the Word

- Go to http://johnhiltoniii.com/guys-girls and look at the resources we've posted for combating pornography. Even if you don't have a problem with pornography, we think the videos and other things we've posted there will strengthen you.
- Take Elder Scott's invitation to sensitively communicate to young women (by your words and actions) that you want them to dress modestly. You can be a great strength to them!

THOUGHTS:
_____
_____

Notes

1. "The Stats on Internet Pornography" on the United Families International Blog (2 June 2010); http://unitedfamiliesinternational.wordpress.com/2010/06/02/14-shocking-pornography-statistics/; accessed 22 December 2010.
2. Ibid.
3. "13.3 Billion U.S. Porn Revenues Exceed Combined Sales of ABC, CBS, and NBC," at NowPublic (May 2008); http://www.nowpublic.com/tech-biz/13-3-billion-u-s-porn-revenues-exceed-combined-sales-abc-cbs-and-nbc; accessed 22 December 2010.
4. *For the Strength of Youth* (Salt Lake City: The Church of Jesus Christ of Latter-day Saints, 2001), 19; emphasis added.
5. Dallin H. Oaks, "Pornography," *Ensign*, May 2005, 90.
6. Spencer W. Kimball, *Spencer W. Kimball* [manual] in Teachings of Presidents of the Church series, (Salt Lake City: The Church of Jesus Christ of Latter-day Saints, 2006), 186.
7. Richard G. Scott, "The Sanctity of Womanhood," *Ensign*, May 2000, 36–37.

- "Pay more attention to us when we dress modestly. Don't drool all over the girls who are immodestly dressed."

- "Take the time in a seminary or Sunday school class to tell us that you appreciate modestly dressed girls."

JOHN—If you find that you are doing this, and girls in your church classes continue to dress inappropriately, then you might consider being more specific. I am not talking about pointing out specific girls, but be more specific about what is immodest.

- "If you have a close relationship with a girl (as a big brother or as a good friend), find a tactful way to let her know that something she is wearing is sending the wrong message. The approach of 'you probably don't realize this, but . . .' may be helpful."

JOHN—As you help young women choose to be modest, you will strengthen them—and yourself. There are other important ways that you can strengthen the young women you know. How? That's the subject of the next chapter.

What *Guys* Need to Know about *Girls*

come down on you, guys. We know that you are doing your best to be warriors. We are sure that *you* are the kind of guy who compliments modestly dressed girls. We hope you can persuade your friends to do the same thing. In fact, all young men have been asked to encourage young women to be modest. Elder Richard G. Scott said, "Young men, let . . . young women know that you will not seek an eternal companion from those that are overcome by worldly trends. Many dress and act immodestly because they are told that is what you want. In sensitive ways, communicate how distasteful revealing attire is to you, a worthy young man, and how it stimulates unwanted emotions from what you see against your will."7

Call to action!

Lani — *Notice how Elder Scott says that in "sensitive ways" we should encourage young women to be modest. So obviously you won't want to do something to make a young lady feel awkward or embarrassed. It may sound crazy, but there have been times when I have gotten ready to leave the house only for my husband to kindly say something like, "Are you sure that is modest?" or "Do you realize this is showing?" The honest truth is that most of the time I had not realized my clothes were revealing at all. I had not intended to dress immodestly. So I am grateful that I have someone who has helped guide me in a way that is not accusatory or condescending. He is still expecting the best of me, but teaching me through a guy's eyes—and it didn't take me long to become a better judge on my own.*

We asked several young women how guys could sensitively encourage them to be modest. Here are some of their responses:

- "Compliment us when we are modestly dressed. You don't have to say 'You look modest' but if you tell us we look pretty when we are dressing modestly, we will want to wear those clothes again."

John — Amen to this! We see young men wearing shirts that say, "MODEST IS HOTTEST," but a personal, specific compliment will go much farther.

taught: "If a young man would not date a young woman who is improperly clothed, the style would change very soon."⁶

Here's the hard truth: Many girls dress immodestly because some guys pay more attention to immodestly dressed girls than to modestly dressed girls. You CAN'T do that! Consider what one young woman told us: "I've noticed that guys are more likely to pay attention to girls who are dressed immodestly. That sends a totally wrong message to those of us who are dressing modestly."

It is interesting that in a priesthood session of conference, Elder Scott essentially asked you young men to take some responsibility for immodesty. However, I hear mixed messages from youth: Guys tell me that they wish girls they knew would dress modestly, but the girls they interact with tell me the guys give all their attention to the immodestly dressed girls. Something is obviously wrong. Either the girls have a false perception, or the guys really do pay more attention to immodestly dressed girls, maybe without realizing it. This is a huge issue for girls. Guys, be fearless and make kind, simple comments that could influence a girl's choice in clothes, possibly for years to come.

JOHN—Another told us, "You need to tell guys how we girls feel when they pay attention to immodestly dressed girls. When boys do that, we start wondering, 'Should I wear shorter shorts so boys notice me?' Sometimes a modestly dressed girl will think, 'Am I doing the right thing? What is wrong with me?' I've known girls that have cried because guys paid all the attention to the immodestly dressed girls. Why would a girl cry because of it? It took courage for her to dress modestly, and then she found out that some boys *go for the immodest girls!* We lose all admiration for boys who act like this."

We aren't trying to

It's important to note that pornography "changes the way you see others." Many young men have reported that after viewing pornography, they see women differently. They start to view them as objects, and that can ruin their relationships with women.

Pornography turns women into objects to be lusted after rather than daughters of God to be cherished. Pornography can rob you of your ability to give proper respect to women and girls.

What have you done to protect yourself from pornography? Do you have filters installed on your computers? Have you put your computer in a room where everyone can see what you are doing? Have you decided beforehand and practiced what you will do when people send you inappropriate e-mails or text messages?

The Church has created some great online resources to help you fight against pornography. We have also created a website at http://johnhiltoniii.com/guys-girls that has links to these and other sites that can help you. Go check them out!

Check it out!

Lani — We know that you don't want to participate in pornography. One of the struggles we face is that pornography is all around us. You even see things you don't want to see, just walking down the halls or even sitting in a class. This is why we want to talk about one aspect of pornography that is all too prevalent—and what you can do to prevent it. It's based on this quote from Elder Dallin H. Oaks, who said to young women: "Please understand that if you dress immodestly, you are magnifying this problem by becoming pornography to some of the men who see you."[5]

Now, don't worry, we're talking to the young women about modesty in their side of this book—but there is something about girls dressing immodestly that *you* need to know. It's *why* they dress this way.

So why do young women dress immodestly? Some say they do it because it is in style. Others say they want to look cute. But the bottom line is that girls want to impress you. President Spencer W. Kimball plainly

Chapter Four

A Topic You Might Not Want to Hear About

JOHN— There is a topic that is frequently discussed (especially among young men), and originally, we weren't going to mention it in this book. But it is a problem so large and ugly that we decided we needed to include it. You've probably already guessed what it is.

Pornography.

Did you know that . . .

- Twelve percent of all websites are pornographic?[1]

- Every second, well over $3,000 is being spent on pornography?[2]

- The worldwide pornography industry has larger revenues than Microsoft, Google, Amazon, eBay, Yahoo!, Apple, and Netflix *combined?*[3]

Yikes.

Pornography is obviously evil, for many reasons. One of them is that viewing pornography can weaken your future marriage! I personally think that is one of the biggest reasons to avoid it like the plague! *For the Strength of Youth* says, "Pornography is a poison that weakens your self-control, *changes the way you see others,* causes you to lose the guidance of the Spirit, and *can even affect your ability to have a normal relationship with your future spouse.*"[4]

JOHN—Okay, warriors—if you weren't convinced before that we should honor young women, we hope you are now. Now we want to talk more about *how* we can honor young women. But first there is a subject we need to talk about—and you might not want to hear about it. You'll see what it is in the next chapter.

- There are many reasons WHY you should honor women. They are <u>S</u>upreme, you will marry one in the <u>T</u>emple, you are <u>A</u>ccountable for how you treat them, <u>N</u>obody lives without them, and our favorite, <u>D</u>uh!

Be Ye Doers of the Word

- Today, show your mom or sister that you honor her as "God's supreme creation" by writing her a kind note or opening the door for her.

- The next time you go to Mutual, give the young women hope by treating each one with genuine respect and kindness.

THOUGHTS:
_____
_____
_____
_____
_____
_____
_____

Notes

1. "Purposes of the Aaronic Priesthood," http://classic.lds.org/pa/ym/DutytoGod_purposes.pdf.
2. Gordon B. Hinckley, "Our Responsibility to Our Young Women," *Ensign*, September 1988, 11.
3. Russell M. Nelson, "Our Sacred Duty to Honor Women," *Ensign*, May 1999, 38.
4. Thomas S. Monson, "That We May Touch Heaven," *Ensign*, November 1990, 47.
5. Hinckley, "Our Responsibility to Our Young Women," 11.
6. *Merriam-Webster's Collegiate Dictionary*, 11th ed. (Springfield, MA: Merriam-Webster, 2008), 829.
7. Joe J. Christensen, "The Savior Is Counting on You," *Ensign*, November 1996, 39.
8. In James R. Clark, comp., *Messages of the First Presidency of The Church of Jesus Christ of Latter-day Saints, 1935–51*, vol. 6 (Salt Lake City: Bookcraft, 1975), 178.

first to get food. I smiled, stepped forward, and simply said, "Thank you." When we were finished getting our food, Jared had gone ahead of me a couple of steps to one of the dining tables to pull out the chair for me. He then gently pushed it to the table when I sat down. Looking back on it, I realize this probably took a little foresight and planning on his part since he let me go ahead of him in line.

Obviously Jared and I were not on a date. This was a family gathering, and I quickly observed that I was not alone in receiving such respect from Jared. I noticed that he ran over to his mother's table and got the chair for her and took her dishes for her when she was done. In fact, Jared showed amazing respect for all the women, young and old, grandmothers and little sisters. He had obviously trained himself to view women with high regard and treat them as such.

At school the next Monday, I sat visiting with five or six friends in journalism class. We often just talked in this class if the school newspaper was done (or not), and they asked me how my weekend was. With a smile and a glow in my eye I said, "It was fabulous. I met a guy I could marry!"

Of course, this got everyone's attention quickly. I made it clear that I did not necessarily mean that I would marry this guy, but that I had finally met a guy who knew how to treat women. It gave me hope that more guys like him might exist somewhere in the world!

I had always associated with "good guys" in seminary and Mutual, and at stake and regional dances, but from what I had seen, they didn't treat girls the way Jared did. It was easy to think that guys like him just did not exist anymore. Although I did not marry Jared (or even date him), I will be forever grateful to him for his bold example of a knight in shining armor. He gave me hope!

of a church class. A rather shy young man told us this: "I have been praying lately to have opportunities to help people during the day. Yesterday I saw a girl during lunch who didn't have a chair, so I gave her my chair! It felt really cool!" We believe that the "cool" feeling he felt was the Holy Ghost testifying to him of the importance of honoring women. As you honor young women you'll feel this too.

Lani — Before we leave this chapter I'd like to add in one more reason for showing respect to young women—it's so you can give them hope! As a teenager, I remember feeling that none of the boys I knew treated me like I wanted my future husband to treat me. When a girl is surrounded by young men who do not even remotely appear to be knights in shining armor, then it is easy to get discouraged and think that no knights in shining armor actually still exist. But one young man bold enough to demonstrate certain acts of chivalry can truly be a <u>beacon of hope</u> to countless girls.   *BE THAT MAN*

That beacon of hope came for me when I was fifteen years old. My sister Angela was planning her wedding and had told me that Jayson, her fiancé, was such a perfect guy. A couple months before the wedding, Angela told me that Jayson had a younger brother who was just two years older than I. She described him as having great musical ability and piercing blue eyes, and that he was just an all-around classy guy.

Well, at fifteen I was not really into the guy scene, but I was excited to meet Jared (the younger brother) when he came to the wedding. I can still picture his family's car pulling into our driveway in San Diego for a family luncheon the day before the wedding in the San Diego Temple. Many of my siblings stood around me on the driveway and greeted the family. When I met Jared, he shook my hand firmly, and confidently looked me in eye. He greeted me with a compliment and a hug. Within thirty seconds of meeting this guy, I felt like a million bucks!

A short time later, Jared and I stood in line by the buffet table. When we reached the food, Jared took a step back and motioned for me to go

Each young man who participated that day felt something special. That "something" was the Holy Ghost testifying to them that they were doing the right thing by honoring women.

JOHN—At another youth conference, we talked just to the young women about the importance of knowing who they really were as daughters of God. Then we spoke to the young men about honoring women. While we were talking to the young men, the young women were in a different building for some other meetings. We ended the meeting with the young men a few minutes early and told them to do something right then to honor the young women.

Lunch was going to be served in the building that the young men were in, so some young men went and began dishing up plates of food so that the young women would have their meals ready-made when they arrived.

Some other young men went outside and discovered that it was raining. They knew that the young women would be arriving in cars, but that they would get wet while they walked from their cars to the chapel. So they went around the chapel and got some plastic garbage bags, and by forming two lines and spreading out the bags they were able to create a dry walkway for the young women to walk under all the way to the chapel.

Lani—We wish you could have seen the faces of those young women when they got back to the chapel. We had told them about who they were as daughters of God, but those young men helped them feel it. As we talked to the young women, they said things like, "These young men have made me feel so special." As we talked to the young men, they said that as they had served the young women, they felt the Spirit. There was a special feeling present that day—we believe it was the Holy Ghost testifying to the young men and the young women that God honors women, and when we do so, we feel of His Spirit more abundantly.

This can be you!

JOHN—You don't have to be at a youth conference for this to happen. We've seen young men simply hold the doors open for young women at the end

What *Guys* Need to Know about *Girls*

Nobody Lives without Them

This reason is pretty self-explanatory. Clearly we should honor women because they are the ones who bring life to the world. The First Presidency of the Church in 1942 wrote: "Motherhood is near to divinity. It is the highest, holiest service to be assumed by mankind. It places her who honors its holy calling and service next to the angels."[8]

Lani—*Motherhood is sacred. Many of the women we interact with are, or will be, mothers at some future time. How would you feel if somebody was using your mother or playing with her heart? You would be horrified! So we, then, have the responsibility to treat other mothers and future mothers with the utmost respect.*

Duh!

John—Okay, so maybe this last reason isn't proper English. But when I hear a young man say, "Why do we have to respect young women?" I'm tempted to say, "Duh! It's obvious!" There are some things that you should just do.

One way that I know it is right and good to honor women is the feeling that comes when I do, and when I see others do so. Once we were at a youth conference, and all of the young men arrived at the cafeteria before the young women did. They could have gone ahead and gotten their food, but instead they decided to do a little surprise for the young women.

They stood in two lines forming a path for the young women to walk down as they entered the cafeteria. As each young woman arrived, the young men burst into applause for her—in effect, giving her a standing ovation. Some of the girls liked it so much they went out of the cafeteria and walked in again!

Lani—*What surprised us the most was that some of the female cafeteria workers (who were not LDS) also walked through the path and received the standing ovation. Later, one of these women expressed, with tears in her eyes, how grateful she felt for the goodness of these young men.*

Isn't that interesting? To neglect God's daughters, all we need to do is give little attention to them or to leave them unattended. In other words, if I don't do anything rude to women, but I ignore them, I am neglecting them. In order to not neglect women, we need to pay attention to them.

For example, I frequently talk to young women and ask them if they could tell me a story about a young man who showed them respect or disrespect. One time, when I asked the question, a young woman's eyes lit up, and she told me about being at a party where ice cream was being served. She was sitting on a couch when a young man brought her a bowl of ice cream.

"I got this for you," he said. "What toppings would you like?" It was a simple thing, but that small act of regard made a big difference!

Consider this story about a brother who did not "neglect" his younger sister.

> A fourteen-year-old sister was all dressed up to go to a Young Women activity at a time in her life when she felt very unsure about herself. She was quietly and self-consciously inching her way toward the front door, hoping not to be noticed by all the young men in the living room who were visiting with her older brother Russell. She was given a life-changing boost when her older brother interrupted his conversation and said to her in front of all his friends, "My, Emily, you look pretty tonight!" A small thing? No. There are young women who claim that they would not have made it through those growing-up years without the encouragement and support of their older brothers.[7]

What a great example! Remember, we're accountable for how we treat women. And that means more than simply not being rude—we need to proactively do more.

And that's one reason we should honor them. Once a young man asked, "What about me—aren't I God's supreme creation?"

We simply said, "No!" ☺

Temple Marriage

Lani—One obvious reason that you should honor women is that you will marry a woman some day. How could you marry somebody for eternity whom you do not respect?

John—Elder Russell M. Nelson said, "You young men need to know that you can hardly achieve your highest potential without the influence of good women, particularly your mother and, in a few years, a good wife. Learn now to show respect and gratitude."[3]

Lani—The Lord has said, "In order to obtain the highest [degree of the celestial kingdom], a man must enter into this order of the priesthood [meaning the new and everlasting covenant of marriage]; And if he does not, he cannot obtain it" (D&C 131:2–3). The fact is, no man returns to live with God without a woman by his side. That is another important reason why we should honor women.

Accountability

John—For me, one of the most serious reasons that men should respect women is that we will be held accountable for how we treat women. Consider the following quotes from modern prophets:

"Men, take care not to make women weep, for <u>God counts their tears</u>."[4] *Whoa!*

"God will hold us accountable if we neglect His daughters."[5]

What does it mean to "neglect" something? Merriam-Webster's Online Dictionary defines "neglect" as "to give little attention or respect; . . . to leave undone or unattended to especially through carelessness."[6]

Priesthood does talk about honoring young women. It says that Aaronic Priesthood holders should "give proper respect to women, girls, and children."[1]

JOHN—We've thought a lot about the question, "Why is it that holders of the Aaronic Priesthood should give proper respect to women, girls, and children?" We'll share with you a partial answer to this question by using the acronym STAND. We chose the word STAND because it reminds us that, in some situations, one way to show respect for women is to STAND when they enter the room.

> **S**upreme Creation
> **T**emple Marriage
> **A**ccountable
> **N**obody Lives without Them
> **D**uh!

Women Are God's Supreme Creation

President Gordon B. Hinckley taught:

> Woman is God's supreme creation. Only after the earth had been formed, after the day had been separated from the night, after the waters had been divided from the land, after vegetation and animal life had been created, and after man had been placed on the earth, was woman created; and only then was the work pronounced complete and good.
>
> Of all the creations of the Almighty, there is none more beautiful, none more inspiring than a lovely daughter of God.[2]

POWER QUOTE

We don't think President Hinckley wanted men to feel depressed or that they are less than women, but some men have the attitude that women are second-class citizens. This is not true. Women are supreme.

Chapter Three

What a Girl Wants

Lani — "What do girls really want?" guys often ask.

Many guys also say, "Girls are so confusing!"

Yes, girls can be confusing, and obviously there are many different types of girls in the world, and no two of them will be exactly alike. But there are some common hopes and dreams that most girls have. Almost every girl you will meet wants to be honored and respected.

John — When we give presentations to young men, we love to talk to them about honoring young women. Often somebody (usually one of the less-mature members of the group) will ask, "Why do we have to honor young women? Why don't they have to honor us?"

The answer to the second question is that, of course, young women should honor young men. I have frequently heard talks encouraging young women to respect young men and help them be their best selves. However, I also noticed that the Young Women theme does not specifically talk about honoring young men.

Lani — Interestingly, though, the stated mission of the Aaronic

> It is pizza night at Mutual, and everybody rushes to the tables until someone shouts, "Ladies first!" But, why *should* ladies be first?

- Be a warrior—protect the women you know. Protect them physically, emotionally, and spiritually.

Be Ye Doers of the Word
- Analyze your actions—are you a player, a hunter, a thief, or a warrior?
- Write down a goal of something you will do to act like a (stripling) warrior. Then do it.

THOUGHTS:
_____
_____
_____
_____
_____
_____
_____
_____
_____
_____

What a great idea! The truth is, being a warrior isn't that hard, and it can be a lot of fun. A lot of it boils down to simply honoring and respecting women. Why should you honor women? That's the topic of the next chapter.

Notes

1. Spencer W. Kimball, *Spencer W. Kimball* [manual], in Teachings of Presidents of the Church series (Salt Lake City: The Church of Jesus Christ of Latter-day Saints, 2006), 181–82.
2. Alexander B. Morrison, *Zion: A Light in the Darkness* (Salt Lake City: Deseret Book, 1997), 91.
3. N. Eldon Tanner, "No Greater Honor: The Woman's Role," *Ensign*, January 1974, 10.
4. James E. Faust, "The Highest Place of Honor," *Ensign*, May 1988, 37.
5. Joshua Harris, *I Kissed Dating Goodbye* (Sisters, OR: Multnomah Publishers, 2003), 99.

What Guys Need to Know about Girls

JOHN — Consider another simple example of a young man who was a warrior. He said:

> I was at the Valentine's Day dance, having a good time with my date, and it came to the last dance of the night. It was a slow dance, and it had just started when I looked over and saw this girl from my seminary class sitting alone in the corner of the room as the music played. I knew she had come to the dance without a date, and she wasn't the most popular girl in school. I wanted my date to have a good time, but I had danced with her all night, and this was the last dance. I felt a strong impression to ask this other girl to dance, so I explained what I was feeling to my date, and she willingly agreed (there was another guy who wanted to dance with her anyway, so it worked out). It's not as though I had any romantic feelings for this girl in the corner, but I could see very clearly that a daughter of God was feeling down on herself—probably feeling unwanted, alone, and rejected on Valentine's Day—and that a simple dance could make her feel better and boost her self-esteem. Her face lit up as I asked her to dance, and I don't regret doing what I did that night. My date thought what I did was really sweet, and she admired me for that; but, more than that, I knew that I had made a daughter of our Heavenly Father know that she was worth something.

Awesome?
☒ ☐
Yes No

Think of it this way—you will not marry all of the girls you know right now. When you see these young ladies in the future, do you want their husbands to thank you or hate you? Joshua Harris wrote, "I want to be the kind of friend to whom girls' future husbands could one day say, 'Thank you for standing watch over my wife's heart. Thank you for guarding her purity.'"5

In other words, if you would do anything to protect your date from physical harm, how much more should you do to protect her from spiritual harm? Just like a warrior would protect his date physically, he guards against doing anything that would harm her spiritually and emotionally. He would never do anything that would compromise her moral purity.

Lani—Now you probably won't have very many times when you have to protect your date from assault. But you will likely have many chances to guard the purity of young women you know. And you will certainly have many, many opportunities as a warrior to protect the self-esteem of the young women you know.

As you date, you will be entrusted by a girl's parents with their most cherished blessing. You will have the responsibility to protect not only her wellbeing, but also her honor, even above your own safety. One of the duties of manhood is to safeguard womanhood.[4]
—President James E. Faust

A real man will protect the women in his life.

It's important that you realize that you don't have to be a super-ninja in order to be the kind of warrior we are talking about. It can be very simple. A young woman said, "A few years ago I was at a church dance and was very upset. A boy that I liked had been stringing me along and telling me how much he liked me. Later, I found out that he was 'dating' someone else. I was so upset, and I was crying in the foyer. A guy I knew gave me a note telling me not to worry because the other boy wasn't worth my time and wasn't good enough for me. I have always remembered that day. I remember feeling so much better as I realized that the particular boy that I thought I liked really wasn't for me."

What **Guys** Need to Know about *Girls*

JOHN—So what do you think of Erik? Clearly, at times in this story he acted like a thief and a player, but based on his apology at the end of his story, it seems as though he wanted to be a warrior.

> There is no surer way for a man to show his lack of character, of good breeding, and of quality than for him to show lack of respect for woman or to do anything that would discredit or degrade her.[3]
> —President N. Eldon Tanner

What do you want to be? Our assumption in writing this book is that you are, or want to be, a warrior! We believe that you are a valiant young man who is truly interested in honoring and respecting young women. We hope that you find this book useful, and that as you read, you take notes of things you can share with your friends to recruit them to your group of warriors.

My friend Adam Miller shared a thought that impressed me, and I think as warriors you'll relate to it. Imagine that you're on a date with a nice young lady from your ward. You are driving to a restaurant where you are going to meet your best friend and his date. As you are walking toward the restaurant, a scary-looking guy approaches you and says, "Step aside, kid!"

Scary guy →

He pushes you and grabs your date.

"Help!" She screams.

What would you do? Your heart would be pounding—there's no doubt about that. I'm sure that the warrior in you would come out—you would want to do whatever it took to protect her. Maybe you'd shout for help; maybe you'd do your best to punch out the other guy; but you would do something.

Now consider how this scenario relates to Matthew 10:28: "Fear not them which kill the body, but are not able to kill the soul: but rather fear him which is able to destroy both soul and body in hell."

I won't lie . . . it seemed to me like it was a magical kiss. I couldn't believe it! But as the dance continued, I started to have an uneasy feeling. I knew that I didn't want to have a relationship with her, but the kiss did feel magical. Would it be wrong to kiss her again?

I called her a few days after the dance and asked her out. I'll be honest, my whole point in asking her out was to kiss her again. As I drove to her house, I was struggling within myself—should I just try to have a good time on the date and not worry about the physical stuff or should I try to make something happen?

When I got to Emily's house, she wasn't quite ready to go. So I talked to her dad for a couple of minutes. It was a fine conversation, but I felt like a rat. If her dad knew what I was planning, he wouldn't like it, I thought. Then I realized, <u>if I were Emily's dad, I wouldn't like it either.</u> *Walk in his shoes.*

So we went on our date. I knew what I wanted to do, and I knew what I had to do. Toward the end of our date, we were sitting next to each other talking. "Listen," I said, "I'm really sorry for what happened at the dance. I don't know what happened, but I know that . . ."

I stopped talking because Emily's eyes were filled with tears. "I feel terrible too," she said. "We hardly even know each other, and we kissed. After the dance I felt so bad."

I didn't know what to say. I apologized, and she did too. Needless to say, we didn't kiss again. Instead I tried to make it a great date for her, and whenever I saw her after that, I tried my best to make her feel comfortable.

What Guys Need to Know about Girls

The Warrior

Finally, there's the warrior. That word might sound scary, but we are, in fact, talking about stripling warriors who are "true at all times" (Alma 53:20). Someday, after serving a faithful mission, the warrior hopes to win the heart of a special young lady. But in the meantime, his focus is on protecting those around him. He wants to uplift and protect the women in his life. At a dance, a warrior has a good time and dances with lots of girls. He looks out for young ladies who haven't been on the dance floor yet and enjoys asking them to dance. If he spots any thieves, he is on guard and is willing to help defend his female friends. You must become a warrior! Elder Alexander B. Morrison said, "Men must learn to act as sons of God rather than as 'natural' men who are the enemies of God. <u>As real men . . . they must honor women.</u>"[2] *[Put on mirror!]*

It's easy to put people into categories, but that's not our point. The fact is, most young men are a blend of these four. Consider this story, told by a young man we'll call Erik. Which is he—a player, a hunter, a thief, or a warrior?

> I was at our stake New Year's Eve dance, and I saw Emily, a girl that I had seen at dances before—but this time she looked totally beautiful. Even though she was two years younger than I was (I was eighteen and she was sixteen), I was definitely interested. We danced together, and I put my arm around her afterward.
>
> I don't remember exactly how it happened. She said something about being my girlfriend—she was just joking around—and I said something like, "If you are my girlfriend, how come we haven't kissed?" And out of nowhere, she kissed me!

all just a game to him. At a dance, his goal might be to dance with the prettiest girls and get as many phone numbers as he can—even though he'll never call most of them.

The Hunter

The hunter knows what he wants and will do anything to get it. To him, a woman's heart is a trophy, and he wants to keep it. Most hunters aren't interested in group dating or dating for fun. A hunter is a conqueror—he wants a conquest! Once he's got her in the bag (as he might say), he doesn't want to let go. The hunter prowls around the dance floor looking for someone he thinks he can capture, so to speak. Once he's found her, he'll try to dance with her all night.

The Thief

The thief is perhaps the most dangerous of these four individuals. He has few morals; he simply takes what he wants and doesn't care who gets hurt. Thieves like to operate in the dark. They insist on privacy, and there is no doubt that hanging out with them leads to big trouble! At a dance, thieves sometimes look for easy targets—young women they think they can take from without any trouble. Sometimes they disguise themselves as players or warriors so that they can rob more easily.

President Spencer W. Kimball described the motivations of the player, hunter, and thief as follows: "The young man is untrue to his manhood who promises popularity, good times, security, fun, and even love, when all he can give is passion and its diabolical fruits—guilt complexes, disgust, hatred, abhorrence, eventual loathing, and possible pregnancy without legitimacy and honor. He pleads his case in love and all he gives is lust."[1]

Be true to your manhood!

Chapter Two

The Player, the Hunter, the Thief, and the Warrior

JOHN—When we speak to groups of young women, we sometimes tell them that there are four types of guys. Which are you?

The Player   The Hunter   The Thief   The Warrior

We're guessing you're a warrior but, just to make sure, let's review these different types of guys.

The Player

First, the player. To this guy, a woman's heart is a toy. He'll smile and flirt, talk and tease, gaze and glance, and do whatever it takes to attract her attention. He's not interested in anything serious, and as soon as he knows a girl likes him, he'll back away. He doesn't really intend to hurt girls (even though he does). It's

- You are a son of God.
- You hold the priesthood of God.
- You are a vital part of a marriage and family.
- God has a work for you to do.

Be Ye Doers of the Word

- Write in your journal about how you feel as an Aaronic Priesthood holder.
- Set a personal goal to help you honor the priesthood you hold.

THOUGHTS:
_____
_____
_____
_____
_____
_____
_____
_____

Bonus Scripture:

"Be strong in the Lord, and in the power of his might."
—Ephesians 6:10

Notes

1. Vaughn J. Featherstone, "The King's Son," *New Era*, November 1975, 35.
2. David A. Bednar, "Becoming a Missionary," *Ensign*, November 2005, 47.
3. *Fulfilling My Duty to God: For Aaronic Priesthood Holders* (Salt Lake City: The Church of Jesus Christ of Latter-day Saints, 2010), 5.
4. "The Family: A Proclamation to the World" (Salt Lake City: The Church of Jesus Christ of Latter-day Saints, 1995).
5. David A. Bednar, "Marriage Is Essential to His Eternal Plan," *Ensign*, June 2006, 83.
6. *Merriam-Webster's Collegiate Dictionary*, 11th ed. (Springfield, MA: Merriam-Webster, 2008), 254.

What *Guys* Need to Know about *Girls*

"The Family: A Proclamation to the World" states, "Gender is an essential characteristic of individual premortal, mortal, and eternal identity and purpose."[4] In many ways the world puts down men today, making them appear incompetent, dumb, or even unnecessary. Worldly philosophies that women are better off without men or that fatherhood is not essential are in stark contrast to what the Lord's prophets are teaching today. Never buy into those blatant lies. When I have had the opportunity to speak to groups of young men decked out in sharp Sunday attire, I have been overcome with the power of good I feel emanating from you. It is overwhelming. I feel of the Lord's love for you and of his confidence and trust in you. It is real. Feel it in your own heart.

"For divine purposes, male and female spirits are different, distinctive, and complementary."[5]
—Elder David A. Bednar

Complement: Something that fills up, completes, or makes perfect.[6]

Lani — When I was in high school I ran track and field. I gave it my all and did well for the couple of months every year that I competed in the 800-meter, the 400-meter and the two-mile races. I served as the president of several clubs throughout those years as well. I felt like my position and responsibilities were important, and, to some extent, they were. But even though I invested hours and sometimes entire days competing at a track invitational or running a club activity, the events were very temporary. My responsibilities lasted no more than a couple of months, and then the glory was given to someone else. This truth of who you are as the seed of Abraham is not temporary. The responsibilities of sharing the gospel and serving with the priesthood will not be removed in a couple of months, or even a couple of years. It is who you are for the rest of your life—even for eternity.

You are part of this "great nation" of Abraham. You are not a trivial person. You were sent to earth at this time to fulfill an important mission for God. When you really understand that, it changes your life.

John — The First Presidency has said directly to young men, "Heavenly Father has great trust and confidence in you and has an important mission for you to fulfill."[3]

Lani — Now, I want you to know that I absolutely *love* being a woman, and I think women are just plain amazing. ☺ But the longer I have been married and the more young men I interact with, the more grateful I have become for men. In a marriage, the female and male attributes complement each other for a greater whole. I have seen this in my marriage. I have become a more complete and better person with a man at my side to counsel with and learn with. There is a necessary component that a man brings to a marriage and a family that is so vital that, when he is gone, it leaves a gaping hole. I shout for joy that Heavenly Father created men! You are a key and essential part of God's plan!

that we are grateful for you and your priesthood duties. We honor what you do and what you bear.

JOHN—Another thing that you young men need to know about yourselves is that you are Abraham's descendants. This means that, in addition to having a divine heritage, you have a royal heritage.

Speaking directly to young men, Elder David A. Bednar said, "You may enjoy music, athletics, or be mechanically inclined, and someday you may work in a trade or a profession or in the arts. As important as such activities and occupations can be, they do not define who we are. First and foremost, we are spiritual beings. We are sons of God and the seed of Abraham."[2]

You are literally a descendant of Abraham. You probably hear people speak about their family history stories; well, here's an important one. Abraham is your ancestor. His story is your family history. The Lord said to Abraham, "I will make of thee a great nation, and I will bless thee above measure, and make thy name great among all nations, and thou shalt be a blessing unto thy seed after thee, that in their hands they shall bear this ministry and Priesthood unto all nations" (Abraham 2:9).

Break free and be the man you can be!

How do you train an elephant? Well, when an elephant is a baby, it is tied to a strong rope attached to an iron stake. The baby elephant tries to break free but can't. In time, the elephant stops trying and believes it can't get away. When the baby grows up, it can easily be controlled by a simple wooden stake. The adult elephant could easily break free, but because it believes it is limited, it doesn't even try. Young men, as priesthood holders, your potential is limitless. Break free of any self-doubts you may have. Break free of your limits! Be the man God knows you can be!

lewd and lusting women. They exposed him to dishonor and distrust. He was surrounded twenty-four hours a day by everything that could drag the soul of a man as low as one could slip. For over six months he had this treatment—but not once did the young lad buckle under pressure. Finally, after intensive temptation, they questioned him. Why had he not submitted himself to these things—why had he not partaken? These things would provide pleasure, satisfy his lusts, and were desirable; they were all his. The boy said, "I cannot do what you ask, for I was born to be a king."[1]

[margin note: So were you!]

In a similar way, you were born to be a king. As a son of God, you have an eternal inheritance. Your Father in Heaven loves you more than you know. One way that you can know of His love and confidence in you is that He has entrusted you with the Priesthood.

David L. Beck, the Young Men general president, once gave a talk entitled "The Magnificent Aaronic Priesthood," in which he emphasized how wonderful your priesthood is. The priesthood you have holds the keys of "the ministering of angels" (D&C 13). Think of it! You have been given God's power. God has so much confidence and faith in you that He has entrusted into your hands the sacred opportunity to represent Him on earth. If God did not believe in you, He would not have entrusted you with the priesthood.

Lani — *One Sunday as I was watching the priests break the bread as the congregation sang the sacrament hymn, I was overcome with gratitude for these young men who make it possible for me and for the whole ward to be blessed by this ordinance. No matter how much I was desirous to personally bless the ward, I realized that I would need to think of ways to bless them other than priesthood ordinances. I realized I could not bless myself with the ordinance of the sacrament. We women want you to know*

Chapter One

What Guys Need to Know about Guys

JOHN— In this book we want to talk to you about what you should know about girls. But first, you have to know a few things about yourself—how great you as a young man really are. Young women hear all the time about how they are daughters of God with a divine mission to fulfill. Do you realize that you are a son of God? Take a moment and really ponder that—what does it mean to be a son of God?

The story is told of the son of King Louis XVI of France:

> King Louis had been taken from his throne and imprisoned. His young son, the prince, was taken by those who dethroned the king. They thought that inasmuch as the king's son was heir to the throne, if they could destroy him morally, he would never realize the great and grand destiny that life had bestowed upon him.
>
> They took him to the tower of the Temple Prison, and there they exposed the lad to every filthy and vile thing that life could offer. They exposed him to foods the richness of which would quickly make him a slave to appetite. They used vile language around him constantly. They exposed him to

James 1:22 says, "Be ye *doers* of the word, and not hearers only" (emphasis added). It's good for you to read this book, but it's even better to act on what you read. At the end of each chapter you will find a "James 1:22 Checklist" with some invitations of things you could do to act on the principles we've discussed in the chapter. Make yourself a better person by *doing* them.

Note

1. M. Russell Ballard, "Conversations—Episode 10"; http://radio.lds.org/eng/programs/conversations-episode-10; accessed 21 December 2010.

What **Guys** Need to Know about *Girls*

JOHN—A common thread in these stories is that they all show how much young women really value and care about what others think about them.

Lani—It's totally true. Guys, you might think it's strange, but we women really care about what guys think of us. A woman who was in her thirties told us about an experience she had when she was twelve years old. Her older brother told her that her tummy was sticking out. Keep in mind that this girl weighed about ninety pounds as a twelve-year-old. She was not fat. But, twenty years later, she remembered that comment and talked about how it still affected her. I have a few brothers, and what they say to me really matters. Several years ago, my older brother Adam came to Miami and stayed in our home for a couple of days. As he was leaving to return to his home in Las Vegas, he said, "Lani, you're doing a great job as a mom." It's been years since he's said it, but I've remembered those words. Coming from my brother, they meant so much to me.

> As you read this book, remember that there are many women in your life. Though the focus in this book is on honoring *young women*, the principles apply to all women you interact with—from young children to the elderly. And they especially apply to your mother, grandmothers, and sisters!

JOHN—We love these words from Elder M. Russell Ballard. He said, "The world needs to see that this church, of all organizations on the face of the earth, honors women."[1] You, as priesthood holders in The Church of Jesus Christ of Latter-day Saints, should honor women the best you possibly can. This book is written directly to you young men on what you need to know about women. A key principle we will discuss is how you can honor young women and make a positive difference in their lives. As you honor and respect women you will find that it changes their lives—and yours.

Brian smiled and said, "I already have!" It was clear that he loved his sister and wanted to do whatever he could to help her have a good time.

Story #2

When one of our daughters was three years old, her aunt Lori sent her a muumuu (a Hawaiian dress) from Hawaii. Shortly afterward, our ward had a Hawaiian luau, and she was so excited to have a real occasion to wear the muumuu. We had a great time, but as we were driving home, our daughter did not look happy.

"What's wrong?" I asked.

In a sad voice, she responded, "Nobody told me I looked beautiful."

It seemed funny to me that she would say that, after all, she was only three. But she was genuinely sad. "Don't worry," I said. "You looked beautiful. I'm sure lots of people thought you were beautiful, and they just forgot to say it."

"Well," our daughter said, "a lot of people saw me, but nobody told me I looked beautiful."

Story #3

Krista was at a dance, and she was not having a good time. She had not been asked to dance all night, and she was seriously wondering if there was something wrong with her. When the last slow song came on, she was walking out of the room when a young man asked her to dance. They had a nice conversation while they danced, and at the end of the song, he escorted her off the dance floor. He looked her in the eyes and said, "Thanks for a lovely dance." He smiled and walked away. It was such a simple thing, but it completely changed Krista's night.

Introduction

JOHN— Hi, guys, my name is John Hilton III.

Lani— And my name is Lani Hilton (the first). John and I were married ten years ago, and for the past few years we've been speaking together to youth about what guys and girls need to know about guys and girls. A key conclusion we discovered is that guys want to know how they should treat young women. We're glad you're reading this book, because we think it sends a signal that you are the kind of young man who wants to treat young women right. We'll begin with three stories.

Story #1

JOHN— One of my heroes of someone who treated women with respect is Brian. He was a young man I met at an EFY program. He was definitely a "cool" kid, and everyone wanted to be with him. I had talked with his younger sister earlier in the week and had discovered that she really looked up to him, and she confided in me that she hoped he would ask her to dance at the dance on Friday.

At the dance I looked for Brian. The dance had been going on for about half an hour when I found him. "Brian," I said, "I think your sister would love it if you'd ask her to dance tonight."

John Hilton III was born in San Francisco and grew up in Seattle. In high school, he played tennis, snowboarded, worked as a lifeguard, and participated in drama productions. He served an LDS mission in Denver, and got a bachelor's degree from Brigham Young University. He earned a master's degree from Harvard and a PhD from BYU, both in education. He has taught seminary and institute and spoken at BYU Education Week and EFY. One lesser-known fact about John is that in high school he won a pizza-eating contest, eating twenty-two pieces of pizza (they were small pieces ☺).

Lani Olsen Hilton is the fifth of twelve children. She was born in Hawaii and grew up in San Diego, California. She graduated from Brigham Young University with a degree in family life education and a minor in music. She loves being married, raising her children, and teaching gospel truths to youth, adults, and children. Some of her favorite high school memories are running cross country, taking a dance class with her mom, hiking Mt. Whitney with her siblings, and leading service clubs.

John and Lani have lived in Boise, Boston, Mexico, Miami, and, currently, Utah. They are the parents of five children.

Contents

Introduction 1

1. What Guys Need to Know about Guys 5
2. The Player, the Hunter,
   the Thief, and the Warrior 11
3. What a Girl Wants 19
4. A Topic You Might Not Want to Hear About 28
5. How to Treat a Young Woman
   Like a Pearl of Great Price 34
6. What about Kissing? 45
7. What Girls Wish Guys Knew 50
8. Potential Pitfalls 59
9. What Should He Do? 68

Conclusion 73

Fun Mutual Night Activity 77

To our children, with love

Illustrations by Bryan Beach; © 2011 Deseret Book

© 2011 John Hilton III and Lani Hilton

All rights reserved. No part of this book may be reproduced in any form or by any means without permission in writing from the publisher, Deseret Book Company, P. O. Box 30178, Salt Lake City, Utah 84130. This work is not an official publication of The Church of Jesus Christ of Latter-day Saints. The views expressed herein are the responsibility of the authors and do not necessarily represent the position of the Church or of Deseret Book Company.

DESERET BOOK is a registered trademark of Deseret Book Company.

Visit us at DeseretBook.com

Library of Congress Cataloging-in-Publication Data
Hilton, John, III, author.
  What guys need to know about girls; what girls need to know about guys / John Hilton III, Lani O. Hilton.
    p. cm.
  Includes bibliographical references.
  ISBN 978-1-60908-054-9 (paperbound)
  1. Man-woman relationships—Religious aspects—The Church of Jesus Christ of Latter-day Saints. 2. Dating (Social customs)—Religious aspects—The Church of Jesus Christ of Latter-day Saints. I. Hilton, Lani, author. II. Title.
  BX8643.Y6H5457 2011
  241'.6765088289332—dc22   2011001900

Printed in the United States of America
Malloy Lithographing Inc., Ann Arbor, Michigan
10   9   8   7   6   5   4   3   2   1

What Guys Need to Know about Girls

John Hilton III
Lani O. Hilton

DESERET BOOK

Salt Lake City, Utah